Discover!
Social Studies

2

GRADE 2
Social Studies

Discover! Social Studies Instructor Guide

Published in Catasauqua, Pennsylvania by Discover Press, a division of Edovate Learning Corp.

334 2nd Street

Catasauqua, PA 18032

edovate.com

Copyright © 2021 Edovate Learning Corp.

All rights reserved. No part of this book may be reproduced or transmitted in any form or by any means, electronic or mechanical, including photocopying, recording, or by any information storage and retrieval system, without permission in writing by the publisher.

ISBN: 978-1-956330-05-2

Printed in United States of America

1st Edition

GRADE 2
Social Studies

Chapter 1

Lesson 1: The World We Live In 5
Lesson 2: Representing Our World 7
Lesson 3: Finding Our Way on a Map 9
Lesson 4: Finding My Country on a Map 11
Lesson 5: The Region Where I Live 13
Lesson 6: Finding Myself on a Map 15
Lesson 7: Exploring Earth's Surface 17
Lesson 8: Features on a Map 19
Lesson 9: **Chapter 1 Review** **21**

Chapter 2

Lesson 10: Communities Around the World 30
Lesson 11: What Makes Communities Special 32
Lesson 12: Community Types 34
Lesson 13: Community Maps 36
Lesson 14: Maps and Travel 38
Lesson 15: Volunteering in a Community 40
Lesson 16: Local Leaders in a Community 42
Lesson 17: Our Government 44
Lesson 18: A Country's Leader 46
Lesson 19: Laws 48
Lesson 20: Elections and Voting 50
Lesson 21: Citizens in a Community 52
Lesson 22: **Chapter 2 Review** **54**

Chapter 3

Lesson 23: What Are Resources? 63
Lesson 24: Goods and Services 65
Lesson 25: Do You Need It? Needs Vs. Wants 67
Lesson 26: Jobs and Income 69
Lesson 27: Budgets and Saving 71
Lesson 28: Taxes 73
Lesson 29: **Chapter 3 Review** **75**

Chapter 4

Lesson 30: The Land Around Us 83
Lesson 31: The Environments of Our World 85
Lesson 32: Adapting to Our Environment 87
Lesson 33: Jobs Around the World 89
Lesson 34: Different Jobs in Different Places 91
Lesson 35: Climate Changes Our Communities 94
Lesson 36: Conserve and Protect
            Natural Resources 97
Lesson 37: Natural Parks of the World 99
Lesson 38: **Chapter 4 Review** **101**

Chapter 5

Lesson 39: What Is Culture? 109
Lesson 40: How Are Cultures Alike
            and Different? 111
Lesson 41: When Cultures Meet 114
Lesson 42: How Immigrants Help
            Their Communities 116
Lesson 43: **Chapter 5 Review** **118**

Chapter 6

Lesson 44: Communities Change Over Time 125
Lesson 45: Conflicts and Cooperation Can Change
            Communities 127
Lesson 46: Changes in Your Community on a
            Timeline 129
Lesson 47: Community Changes From the Past
            to Present 131
Lesson 48: Community Conflict and Cooperation .. 133
Lesson 49: Timeline for the Community 135
Lesson 50: How Communities Have Changed 137
Lesson 51: **Chapter 6 Review** **139**

GRADE 2
Social Studies

Chapter 7

Lesson 52: Indigenous People 146

Lesson 53: Indigenous People in Your Area 148

Lesson 54: Indigenous Natural Resources 150

Lesson 55: Indigenous People's Food 152

Lesson 56: Culture of Indigenous People 154

Lesson 57: Art of Indigenous People 156

Lesson 58: Folklore From the
Indigenous People 158

Lesson 59: Artifacts of Indigenous People 160

Lesson 60: Indigenous People
Around the World 162

Lesson 61: Natural Resources Used by
Indigenous People 164

Lesson 62: What Indigenous People Ate 166

Lesson 63: How Indigenous People Live 168

Lesson 64: Comparing Culture to That of
Indigenous People 170

Lesson 65: Folklore of Indigenous People 172

Lesson 66: Comparing Artifacts to Those of
Indigenous People 174

Lesson 67: Comparing and Contrasting
Indigenous Peoples 176

Lesson 68: Sites and Monuments of
Indigenous Cultures 178

Lesson 69: **Chapter 7 Review** **180**

Chapter 8

Lesson 70: Explorers 187

Lesson 71: An Explorer's Journey 189

Lesson 72: This Land Is Your Land 191

Lesson 73: Owning Land 193

Lesson 74: Explorers and Indigenous People 195

Lesson 75: Arrival of Explorers 197

Lesson 76: Remembering Explorers 199

Lesson 77: **Chapter 8 Review** **201**

LESSON 1
The World We Live In

Lesson Objectives

By the end of this lesson, your student will be able to:
- identify the continents and oceans of the world
- find the continents and oceans on a globe
- locate the North Pole, South Pole, equator, longitude lines, and latitude lines on a globe

Supporting Your Student

Explore
If you have access to a globe, allow your student to use the globe so they can feel it and touch it. If you don't have access to a globe, you could use a balloon or a ball to help your student understand the three-dimensional qualities of a globe. This will help your student understand that globes are different from maps because they do not lie flat. Make sure to give your student enough time to observe and discover on their own. If your student is having some trouble coming up with observations or questions, ask some guiding questions like "Do you notice different colors? Why do you think there are different colors?," "What do we usually color blue?," or "Do you notice any words?"

Read
If your student has difficulty retaining the meaning of the vocabulary in this lesson, stop and have them go back and touch the representation of each vocabulary word on a map and/or a globe. For example, if your student struggles with remembering what the word "equator" means, have them go back and read the definition again. Then, allow them to trace their finger along the equator on a world map and/or a globe.

Practice
If your student is struggling with drawing and labeling longitude lines, latitude lines, or the equator, have them first go back to the text and read each definition. Then, have your student draw or color the item on the globe before moving onto the next item. Breaking apart this activity into simpler steps can help your student better retain the content.

Learning Styles

Auditory learners may enjoy making a song to help remember the names of the oceans and continents.

Visual learners may enjoy creating a memory game that matches a picture of each continent or ocean with its corresponding name.

Kinesthetic learners may enjoy forming their body into various features of the globe and having their family guess which feature they are representing. For example, your student may hold their arms out wide, as if holding a large ball, to show that their arms are forming the equator.

Extension Activities

Make Your Own Flash Cards
Because this lesson is so rich in vocabulary, it is a great chance for your student to make flash cards! Help your student draw or glue a picture representing each vocabulary word in this lesson on the front side of an index card. Then, write the corresponding vocabulary on the back side of the index card. Your student can make a game out of teaching other members of the family the new vocabulary they have learned.

Around the Globe Game
Ask your student to make a list of questions about the globe and the concepts learned in this lesson. Use those questions to make a trivia game to play together.

Discover! SOCIAL STUDIES • GRADE 2 • LESSON 1

LESSON 1
The World We Live In

Answer Key

Explore

Answers may vary. Possible answers: It is mostly colored blue. There are many different colors on it like blue, yellow, orange, etc. One of the globes has a thick, orange line around it. There are black lines that go all around the globe. The colors might show land and water. I wonder why there are black lines on the globe.

Write *(Write down the names of the oceans and the continents on the lines below.)*

Oceans	Continents
1. Atlantic	1. Africa
2. Arctic	2. Antarctica
3. Indian	3. Asia
4. Pacific	4. Australia
5. Southern	5. Europe
	6. North America
	7. South America

Show What You Know

1.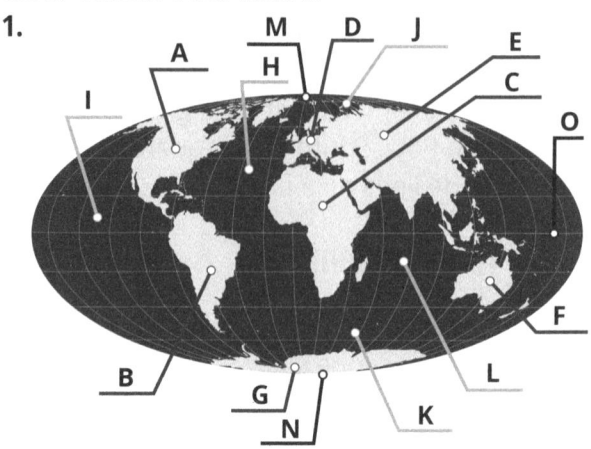

2. longitude lines
3. latitude lines

Practice

Horizontal (latitude) lines should be blue; vertical lines (longitude) should be green; the North Pole should be colored red; the South Pole should be colored orange

LESSON 2
Representing Our World

Lesson Objectives
By the end of this lesson, your student will be able to:
- identify the different ways we can show what our world looks like
- compare and contrast a globe and a map
- find the continents and oceans on a map
- locate the equator, latitude lines, and longitude lines on a map

Supporting Your Student

In the Real World
You can practice the understanding of a bird's eye view by asking your student to look at an object from above. For example, a can would look like a circle from above but like a rectangle if you look at it from the side. Ask them to stand up and look at their chair or their desk from a standing position. What shape do they see?

Explore
Your student who struggles with coming up with similarities and differences between a globe and a map may benefit from you thinking aloud about one similarity or difference that you notice. You could choose a similarity or difference that is less obvious and will encourage them to pay close attention to detail. For example, you might note that the continent of Africa looks curved on the globe while it looks like a slightly different shape on the map.

Read (How Can We Show the Earth?)
Help your student understand how a flat map might distort the shape or size of something that is round. Roll clay or dough into a ball. Have your student use a marker to draw a dot on the ball. Then, flatten the ball. Guide your student to observe how the dot looks after the ball is flattened. Emphasize that this is similar to how continents and other objects on a map might look different than they would on a globe or a three-dimensional picture of Earth. By taking something that is round and making it flat, the size and dimensions of the object may be altered.

Practice
To help your student create their map, encourage them to complete the steps one at a time and to mark off each step as they complete it. In Step 1, if your student is struggling to identify the continent that is missing, encourage them to look at the maps on the previous pages. Prompt your student to compare those maps to the map they are creating while focusing on what is missing. In Step 3, encourage your student to use a ruler or other straight edge to help them draw lines of latitude and longitude.

Learning Styles
Auditory learners may enjoy singing songs about the seven continents. You can find many options available online.

Visual learners may enjoy drawing a world map themselves, coloring it, and adding other artistic touches to it.

Kinesthetic learners may enjoy putting together puzzles of maps or making a map using building blocks.

Extension Activities

Making Connections With Maps
Using a world map, have your student find, label, and color the place where they live. Then your student can find places where other family members or friends live. They can also find places they have traveled to and places they would like to go to.

History of Cartography
Ask your student the following questions: How do you think people created maps of the world before there were airplanes or aircrafts that could fly way above the Earth? How do you think they knew what the shapes of the different places on Earth were without the advantage of having a bird's eye view? Research with your student the history of cartography. Have them create a poster or oral presentation to share their research with a friend or family member.

LESSON 2
Representing Our World

Answer Key

Explore
Answers may vary. Possible answers:
- Maps: flat, you can see the whole world at once, light, easy to carry
- Globe: round, can spin, you can't see the whole world at once
- Both: they have colors, they have words on them, they are models of Earth, they show the continents, they show the oceans

Write *(When would you use a map? When would you use a globe?)*
Answers may vary. Possible answers: A globe is a more accurate representation of Earth because it is round, but a map is easier to carry and can be printed in books. You can make maps more detailed because you can zoom into one area and show it with more detail. You would use a globe when you want to see things in a more accurate way because a map distorts size and shape in order to make everything from a round surface into a flat surface. It is easier to take a map with you than a globe when you are traveling.

Write *(What information can you learn about the world from the map above?)*
Answers may vary. Possible answers: I can find what countries the equator crosses through. I can find how far one place in the world is from another by using latitude and longitude lines.

Practice

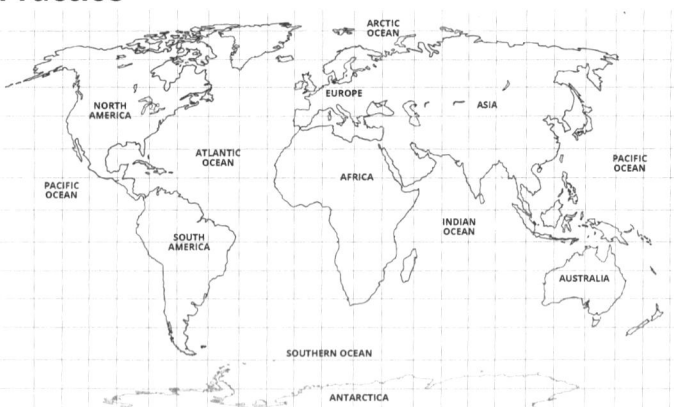

Color of continents may vary.

Show What You Know
1. maps, globes
2. Answers may vary. Possible answers: Globes are round and maps are flat. Globes are a more accurate representation of Earth than maps.
3. Answers may vary. Possible answers: They are both models of Earth, they have longitude and latitude lines, and they show the same places.
4. north to south
5. east to west
6. A. orange
   B. brown
   C. yellow
   D. red
   E. blue
   F. green
   G. purple
7. A. 5
   B. 1
   C. 4
   D. 2
   E. 3

LESSON 3
Finding Our Way on a Map

Lesson Objectives

By the end of this lesson, your student will be able to:

- identify a compass rose on a map and the cardinal directions shown
- identify directions on a map using a compass rose
- locate the cardinal directions using north as a reference point
- identify the abbreviations for the four cardinal directions
- determine the relative location of an object or place

Supporting Your Student

Explore
Allow your student to have some time observing the map. If your student has trouble answering the questions, ask them to think of a time when they used a map in real life. Discuss what the different symbols on the map represent and how they could be useful when lost. For example, if you know the blue line represents a river, you could find the river in the park and follow it until you reach another destination.

Read *(Cardinal Directions on a Compass Rose)*
This lesson is about the cardinal directions: north, south, east, and west. Have your student try to figure out where these cardinal points are in relation to your house. Where is the north side of your house? Where is the south side? East? West? Help your student find the cardinal points in the room where you are. If possible, label each wall with the letters N, E, W, and S. Go outside in the morning to find the sun in order to find east. Ask your student, "If that direction is east, then where is north?"

Read *(What Is Relative Location?)*
As your student reads this informational text, help them notice that there are photographs and illustrations that can help them better understand what they are reading. The images can help add meaning to the words. For example, they can compare what they read about the relative location of North America with the map provided to assist with comprehension. Have them touch the United States and move their finger up to Canada. Relate this movement to the direction that north is pointing on the compass rose. Then they can move their finger to the south to find Mexico, to the west to find the Pacific Ocean, and to the east to find the Atlantic Ocean.

Learning Styles

Auditory learners may enjoy playing a game of Simon Says using the cardinal directions. Prior to the game, establish which way is north, south, east, and west given your current location. When you play the game, your student should move to the location that you say aloud—but only what Simon says! For example, if you say, "Simon says move east", your student should move in that direction.

Visual learners may enjoy drawing a map of their house, making sure to include a compass rose.

Kinesthetic learners may enjoy dancing to and singing popular line dance songs and substituting directional words, such as front, back, right, and left with north, south, east, and west.

Extension Activities

Use Maps in the Real World
Encourage your student to use maps when going to different places in your community. Use a combination of paper and digital maps. Have them identify the direction you are traveling using the compass rose on the map.

Map Your Neighborhood
Create a map of your neighborhood with your student. You might want to go for a walk to make a list of places to include. Be sure to include a compass rose.

LESSON 3
Finding Our Way on a Map

Answer Key

Explore
Answers may vary. Possible answers: It could be useful if I could find some of the items on the map in the real world. If I saw where the lake was in real life, I could find it on the map. Then I could see where to go. It is missing directions. It doesn't show where north is. It would be hard to know which direction to go in real life.

Write *(Move the Mouse)*
<u>four</u> spaces <u>west</u>

<u>two</u> spaces <u>south</u>

<u>one</u> space <u>east</u>

Practice
1. south
2. north
3. east
4. west

Show What You Know
1.
2. west
3. south
4. north
5. east
6. To get to 1, the bee moves <u>two</u> spaces <u>north</u>. To get from 1 to 2, the bee moves <u>four</u> spaces <u>west</u>. To get from 2 to 3, the bee moves <u>three</u> space <u>south</u>. To get from 3 to 4, the bee moves <u>two</u> space <u>east</u>.
7.

N	→	north
E	→	east
W	→	west
S	→	south

LESSON 4
Finding My Country on a Map

Lesson Objectives
By the end of this lesson, your student will be able to:
- identify their country on a map
- describe what is to the north, south, east, and west of their country

Supporting Your Student

Read
If your student is struggling to find country labels, bordering countries, or bordering oceans, encourage them to use their finger to pass over the page until they find the label they are looking for. Also, help your student notice the trends in each map. You can prompt them with questions like "How does this map show country borders?" and "How does this map show bodies of water?" This will help your student decipher the patterns of how each map shows key features such as country labels, country borders, and bodies of water.

Write (What continent and country do you live in?)
To help your student find their continent and country, use a map or globe. Have your student first locate the larger section of land where their country is located. Remind your student that this larger section is a continent just like the continents displayed on the first map in the Explore section. Then have your student find their country on the continent. Emphasize that their country is a smaller part of the larger continent. Have your student trace the borders of their country to distinguish it from the surrounding areas.

Practice
For this activity, use a map or globe to guide your student in finding their country. After your student has located their country, review the compass rose that may be on the map or globe. Guide your student to place their finger on their country and then move it north, south, east, and west. Whatever land or water their finger moves to will indicate what is north, south, east, or west of their country. Explain that sometimes there might be multiple countries that border a country.

Learning Styles

Auditory learners may enjoy creating a video about their country and the oceans and countries that border it. They could do some research about the oceans and countries and talk about these facts and how the bordering countries might interact with their country.

Visual learners may enjoy drawing and coloring a picture of their country and the countries and/or water features that border it. Then they can trace the borders of their country with glue and sprinkle glitter onto the border to make it stand out.

Kinesthetic learners may enjoy creating a matching game with an outline of a world map and the names of the different countries and oceans.

Extension Activities

Learn About Other Countries
What other countries are significant to your student? Was your student born in a different country? Did their ancestors come from another country? Do they have family members living in a different country? Find these other countries on the map and figure out what borders them to the north, east, west, and south. Guide your student to research some other interesting facts about these bordering countries or oceans.

Interview a Friend or Neighbor
To encourage your student to both learn about and appreciate other cultures, help them create a short list of interview questions to ask a friend or neighbor who either immigrated from another country or who is closely tied to their ancestral roots in another country. Questions might include "What countries border the country where you were born?," "What do you wish people would know about the country where you were born?," and "If I were to go and visit, what would you recommend that I be sure and see?" These last two questions might help your student see the study of countries as exciting. Your student might start to realize that every country is home to actual people with interesting stories to tell.

LESSON 4
Finding My Country on a Map

Answer Key

Write *(What continent and country do you live in?)*
Answers may vary depending on your student's country.

Write *(What can surround or border a country?)*
Countries can be surrounded by other countries as well as oceans and seas.

Practice
Answers will vary depending on the country where you live.

Show What You Know
Answers will vary depending on the country where your student lives.

LESSON 5
The Region Where I Live

Lesson Objectives

By the end of this lesson, your student will be able to:

- state the meaning of the word *region*
- identify ways people can divide the world into regions
- identify characteristics of the region where your country is located

Supporting Your Student

Read

As your student reads about regions, emphasize that there are many ways to group areas into regions. To illustrate this, give your student an assortment of small objects like toys or buttons. Have your student sort the objects based on a similar characteristic, such as color or size. This is similar to creating regions. All the objects in a group have a similar characteristic just like all the areas in a region have something in common. Then have your student sort the objects based on another similar characteristic. The same objects may now be in different groups. In the same way, areas may be grouped together differently depending on what they have in common. For example, parts of Russia and Canada may be in the same region for climate reasons because they are very cold. They may not be in the same region based on the languages spoken because different languages are spoken in each country.

Many times the regions will stay the same. For example, regions that are based on location, like the Northeast region of the United States, never change because the states do not move. However, regions based on cultural aspects like language and religion can change over time. This depends on the movement of people from one area to another. If the main language or religion in a country or area changes, then the region it belongs to would change as well.

Write

To help your student answer the Write sections, have them find the continent their country is located on. Then have them identify the color(s) they see. Encourage them to look at the map key that shows what region the color represents.

Practice

Assist your student with describing the regions their country may be a part of by referring to the climate and biome maps in the lesson. To determine the most popular language and religion of your country, assist your student in researching this information using online or print resources.

Learning Styles

Auditory learners may enjoy having a discussion with you about how different areas of the world are the same or different. You can use the maps in the lesson to guide the discussion.

Visual learners may enjoy re-creating the climate or biome map using different materials, such as paint, chalk, or pastels.

Kinesthetic learners may enjoy making a copy of the US map from the lesson and cutting it up to make a puzzle of the different geographic regions. Then they can put the puzzle together to show all the geographic regions in the United States.

Extension Activities

Regions of Your House

Have your student draw a map of their house and divide it into regions. They could base their regions off what activities are done in each area (i.e., eating, sleeping, relaxing) or another similar characteristic.

Regions of Your Town or City

Have your student look at a map of their town or city. Ask them to think about how they would divide the area into regions. Some examples of characteristics they could use to create regions could be:

- open areas of land and areas with a lot of buildings and development
- areas where people live, areas where people work, and areas where people play
- areas where many people live and areas where few people live

LESSON 5
The Region Where I Live

Answer Key

Explore
Areas with the same colors have the same types of land and water.

Write *(Name the climates in the continent you live in.)*
Answers will vary depending on the continent your student lives in.

Write *(Name the biomes in the continent you live in.)*
Answers will vary depending on the continent your student lives in.

Practice
Answers will vary depending on your student's country.

Show What You Know
1. C
2. False
3. A, B, C
4. B

LESSON 6
Finding Myself on a Map

Lesson Objectives
By the end of this lesson, your student will be able to:
- identify their personal location on a map, including the country and continent of origin
- locate what is to the north, south, east, and west of their current location
- explain why it is important to know their location in the world

Supporting Your Student

Read *(Where in the World Do I Live?)*
If your student struggles with the activities on this page, ask your student to name any of the continents that they can remember. Use a globe or map to review the different continents and countries with the student. Have your student point to each continent and name it. Guide your student to find their continent and then their country.

Practice
Help your student determine what is north, south, east, and west of their country using a map. First, have them point to their country. Then, move up (north), down (south), right (east), and left (west). As they move across the map, have them recognize the countries or bodies of water around them. Point out that some bigger countries might have more than one country that borders them on any side.

Write *(List one reason why it is important to know your personal location.)*
To help with brainstorming why knowing one's location is important, it could be helpful to discuss this topic with your student before writing. Ask your student to think about how they would feel if they were lost. They would want to know where they are and what is around them so they can find their way back. This is one reason knowing your personal location is important. Guide them to see that knowing their location also helps them make decisions. For example, they can check a weather report for their area to see what type of clothes they should wear.

Learning Styles
Auditory learners may enjoy finding places on a map following oral directions using cardinal directions.

Visual learners may enjoy looking at aerial photographs of their neighborhood to identify the places around them.

Kinesthetic learners may enjoy taking a walking tour around the neighborhood in the different cardinal directions to find the places around them.

Extension Activities

What Is Your Location Game?
Create a map game to practice identifying a location with your student. Have them close their eyes and put their finger on a point on a world map. Wherever a player lands on the map, they should identify places to the north, south, east, and west of that location. Players should also identify the continents where they land.

Treasure Map
Hide a treasure in your neighborhood and create a map for your student to find it. Make sure the map has a compass rose so your student can practice using cardinal directions in the real world.

LESSON 6
Finding Myself on a Map

Answer Key

Write *(Fill in the blanks using the map above to help you.)*
Answers will vary depending on your student's location.

Practice
Answers will vary depending on your student's location.

Write *(List one reason why it is important to know your personal location.)*
Answers may vary. Possible answers: To help you find other locations. To have a better understanding of the land, water, and weather. To help you make plans.

Show What You Know
1. B
2. stoplight
3. police station
4. store
5. road
6. Answers will vary depending on your student's continent.
7. Answers will vary depending on your student's country.
8. True

LESSON 7
Exploring Earth's Surface

Lesson Objectives

By the end of this lesson, your student will be able to:

- state the meaning of the word *landform*
- identify characteristics of different landforms and bodies of water
- identify common landforms and bodies of water on a map

Supporting Your Student

Read

Encourage your student to connect the content in this lesson with some of their real-life experiences. Ask your student if they have seen some of these landforms in real life. Some of the terms might be more familiar to your student, like mountain, hill, or island, where some others might be new. Your student might need more help understanding these concepts. Ask your student to look at the photographs and describe what they see before they read the text. This will help them engage their own existing knowledge on the topic.

Write *(Choose a landform or body of water. Describe what it looks like.)*

Before your student completes the Write section, make sure they understand and can describe each landform or body of water. One way to support your student with understanding the landforms and bodies of water is by drawing simple pictures of each landform or body of water. For example, draw a circle and color the inside of the circle blue. Then, color around the circle in brown. This is water surrounded by land. It is a lake. You can then draw a brown circle surrounded by blue. This landform surrounded by water is an island.

Practice

If your student struggles figuring out which landform or body of water is represented by each number on the map, suggest that they start by looking for an ocean since they learned about them in a previous lesson. You can remind them that blue on the map represents water. You could also ask them leading questions like "Do you see a body of water that is surrounded by land? What do you call a body of water surrounded by land?" or "Do you see a landform surrounded by water? What do you call a landform surrounded by water?"

Learning Styles

Auditory learners may enjoy recording themselves explaining the landforms and bodies of water and listening to it again.

Visual learners may enjoy drawing simple graphic symbols to represent each of the landforms and bodies of water, such as drawing triangles to represent mountains.

Kinesthetic learners may enjoy coming up with gestures to represent each of the landforms and bodies of water. Examples include raising their arms over their head in a triangle for a mountain or extending their arms in a circle in front of them to represent a lake.

Extension Activities

Landforms Album

Your student can look for images of the different landforms and bodies of water in magazines, newspapers, brochures, or advertising pages and create an album with these pictures. Remind them to label the images. Encourage your student to collect more images as they find them. If possible, identify where these landforms are located. Your student can also look for images to print online.

Memory Game

Make a memory game that matches photos or illustrations of different landforms with their names. Play with your student.

LESSON 7
Exploring Earth's Surface

Answer Key

Explore
Answers will vary. Possible answers: bumpy, wet, dry, hot in some spots, cold in other places

Write *(Choose a landform or body of water. Describe what it looks like.)*
Answers will vary. Possible answers: A mountain is made of rock and rises high above the land and has a peak. A valley is the land between two mountains. A hill rises above the land but is shorter than a mountain. An island is land surrounded by water. An ocean is a large body of salt water. A lake is a body of water surrounded by land. A river is water that flows across land into a larger body of water.

Practice
1. ocean
2. mountains
3. lake
4. island

Show What You Know
5. E
6. D
7. C
8. B
9. A
10. B
11. 1. island
    2. ocean
    3. lake
    4. mountains

LESSON 8
Features on a Map

Lesson Objectives
By the end of this lesson, your student will be able to:
- locate and identify physical and human features shown on a map
- identify physical features of the country you live in

Supporting Your Student

Read
Your student will be practicing the skill of reading maps in this lesson. Assist your student in seeing that the maps show the names of oceans, lakes, rivers, and mountains. Prompt your student to notice that the different colors represent different things. Have them point to each feature as they read, describe it as a physical or human feature, and then say what it looks like on a map. For example, they might point to a mountain and say, "Mountains are physical features. They can be brown on a map."

Write *(What is the difference between physical and human features?*
Have your student think about where physical and human features come from as a way to think about how they are different. Ask guiding questions, such as "Would physical features be here if people were never on Earth?" and "Would human features be here if people were never on Earth?"

Practice
Have maps of your region or country available for your student to explore. You can use paper maps or find maps online. Ask your student to look outside and name some things they see that were made by humans and some things that are from nature. This can help them to experience these features in a concrete way.

Learning Styles

Auditory learners may enjoy creating and answering riddles where the answers are the different physical and human features found on maps.

Visual learners may enjoy finding images of different physical and human features in magazines or online and comparing them to each other.

Kinesthetic learners may enjoy going on a walk around the neighborhood and identifying physical and human features around them.

Extension Activities

Travel Brochure
Your student can create a travel brochure of their country or region describing the physical and human features to visit. The brochure could include a map of the area that shows these features, as well as information about them.

Pros and Cons of Human Features
Humans have built many things that have changed the surface of Earth. Brainstorm with your student some of the positive and negative effects of these human features. For example, building a road may help people get around to different places quicker; however, it also might displace animals or destroy plants that lived in the area where the road was built.

LESSON 8
Features on a Map

Answer Key

Take a Closer Look
The lights come from something that is made by people.

Explore
Answers may vary. Possible answers:

(Same) Both have trees and water

(Different) The first picture has buildings and a bridge and the second does not. The second picture has mountains and the first does not.

(Sidebar) From nature: mountains, river, trees
Made by people: buildings, bridge, roads

Write *(What is the difference between physical and human features?)*
Answers may vary. Possible answer: Physical features are from nature and human features are made by people.

Practice
Answers will vary depending on your student's country.

Show What You Know
1. A
2. B
3. H: roads
   P: rivers
   H: buildings
4. A, C, D
5. Answers will vary depending on your student's country.

LESSON 9
Chapter 1 Review

Lesson Objectives

By the end of this lesson, your student will review the following big ideas from Chapter 1.

- We live on a round planet called Earth that is made of land and water. (Lesson 1)
- Globes and maps are models of Earth that help us understand it better. (Lesson 2)
- There are four cardinal directions that help us describe the location of different places on Earth. (Lesson 3)
- There are different countries on Earth. (Lesson 4)
- There are many different regions on Earth. (Lesson 5)
- It is important to know my location on Earth. (Lesson 6)
- The surface of Earth is covered with different landforms and bodies of water. (Lesson 7)
- Maps can show the different physical and human features of a region. (Lesson 8)

Supporting Your Student

Review *(Our Planet Earth)*
As your student reads this section, reinforce that people divide up Earth in different ways to help them make sense of the world. For example, they first divide up the world by continents and oceans. This helps people to understand the large sections of land and water found on our planet. Next, people divide these larger pieces of land into countries. Over time, people have organized different sections of each continent into countries that share a common government and identity. Finally, people try to see the similarities and differences between countries by grouping them into regions. Countries and smaller areas of land, like states, cities, and towns, can be grouped into regions based on many different common attributes like location, climate, biomes, religion, and language.

Write *(Write the names of the continents and oceans.)*
As your student writes down the names of the continents and oceans, have them touch the continent or ocean on the map and say the name. This can help them to remember not only the names of the continents and oceans but also their location in the world.

Practice *(Our Earth Words)*
If your student struggles with identifying the word that does not belong, practice with a couple of easier examples of this activity. You can tell them three words like *cat*, *dog*, and *house* and ask them, "Which one does not belong in the group? Why?" Then help your student apply this principle to the vocabulary words. For example, you might comment that for the group *north, down, east, west*, you noticed some of those words on the compass rose. Have your student find *north, east,* and *west* on the compass rose before asking them if *down* is on the compass rose as well. Guide your student to see that *down* is not a cardinal direction found on the compass rose. Therefore, it does not belong in the group.

Practice *(Comparing Maps and Globes)*
To assist your student with this activity, it may be helpful to have a map and globe available for them to look at while filling in the Venn diagram.

Learning Styles

Auditory learners may enjoy coming up with their own groups of words where one of them does not belong in the group using vocabulary from this chapter. They might also enjoy saying these word groups aloud to see if a friend or family member can find the word that does not belong.

Visual learners may enjoy using different colors of pencil or pen when filling out the different sections of the diagrams and charts in this lesson. This will help your student have a visual clue to what items are the same and different.

Kinesthetic learners may enjoy writing their ideas for the Venn diagram on sticky notes and moving the pieces around into groups on a table or wall to show similarities and differences.

Extension Activities

An Edible Globe Activity
Use an orange or mandarin as a model of Earth.

LESSON 9
Chapter 1 Review

Have your student hold it and think of which parts of the orange would represent the North and South Poles. Peel the orange and notice how it is divided in sections and make the connection to longitude lines. You can also cut it in half to show the two hemispheres—North and South. Talk about these words, explaining that Earth is a sphere and half of a sphere is called a hemisphere. The best part of the activity is that you get to enjoy eating this model of Earth at the end!

Make a Map of a Park
Visit a park in your community. Have your student create a map of the park, including physical features and human features. Ask your student to use different colors to represent different items on the map. Ask your student to add a map key that explains what each color and graphic on the map represents.

Answer Key

Write *(Write the names of the continents and oceans.)*

1. Africa
2. Antarctica
3. Asia
4. Australia
5. Europe
6. North America
7. South America

1. Arctic Ocean
2. Atlantic Ocean
3. Indian Ocean
4. Pacific Ocean
5. Southern Ocean

Practice *(Our Earth Words)*
Possible answers shown for your student's explanation:

1. down: The other words are *cardinal directions*. Down is not a cardinal direction.
2. mountain: A mountain is a landform. The other words are *bodies of water*.
3. island: An island is a physical feature found in nature. The other words are *human features*.
4. Canada: Canada is a country. The other words are *continents*.
5. compass rose: A compass rose shows the directions of north, south, east, and west. The other words are *imaginary lines* that divide the world.

Practice *(Comparing Maps and Globes)*
Answers may vary. Possible answers:

(Globes) looks like a sphere or ball, more accurate

(Maps) flat, can show just one part of Earth in more detail

(Both) models of Earth; have latitude and longitude lines; show oceans, continents, and countries

Practice *(Features of Earth)*
Answers may vary. Possible answers:

Landforms: mountain, valley, hill, island

Bodies of water: ocean, lake, river

Human features: cities, roads, lighthouses, bridges, tunnels, streets, houses, buildings

CHAPTER 1
Assessment

Quick Review

Refer to the statement your student circled in the Show What You Know section to self-assess their knowledge of the chapter concepts. Then to assist in determining if your student is ready to take the assessment, consider:

- Having your student explain the similarities and differences between a map and a globe.
- Having your student identify the seven continents and five oceans on a map.
- Having your student give examples of landforms, bodies of water, and human features.

CHAPTER 1
Assessment

Chapter Assessment

Project: Audio Recording

Project Requirements or Steps:

An audio recording is a recording of sound. For this project, create an audio recording of a speech, story, or conversation that relates to the chapter. Be sure to include information about at least **one** of the following topic areas from the chapter:

- Globes and maps and how they are the same or different
- The names of continents and oceans
- Cardinal directions and how they can help you find your way
- Examples of human and physical features
- Examples of landforms and bodies of water

CHAPTER 1
Assessment

Chapter Assessment Rubric

Use the following rubric to grade your student's assessment.

	4	**3**	**2**	**1**	**Points**
Creativity	The audio recording is very creative and goes above and beyond expectations.	The audio recording is creative and meets expectations.	The audio recording has one or two creative elements.	The audio recording is not creative.	
Content	The content of the audio recording is very informative, very interesting, and related to the unit.	The content of the audio recording is informative, related to the unit, and interesting.	The content of the audio recording is somewhat informative and only slightly related to the unit.	The content of the audio recording is not informative and not related to the unit.	
Audio	The audio is clear and easy to understand. The speaker is loud and pronounces everything correctly.	The audio is clear, but there are a few times when the speaker does not pronounce everything correctly.	The audio is somewhat unclear and the speaker stumbles frequently.	The audio cannot be understood or the speaker is unable to convey his or her point.	
Grammar and Mechanics	The audio recording contains no grammatical errors.	The audio recording has one or two grammatical errors, but they do not take away from understanding the content.	The audio recording has several grammatical errors, and they sometimes take away from understanding the content.	The audio recording has too many grammatical errors to be understood.	

Total Points ____/16

Average ____

CHAPTER 1
Assessment

Alternative Assessment

It is recommended that the instructor provides the student with support during the assessment to include reading and explaining directions, reading any unknown words or phrases, allowing the student to provide verbal responses that are then recorded, and allowing the student to complete sections of the assessment over the course of the day(s).

1. Use the words in the Word Bank to label the continents and oceans on the map.

Word Bank: Africa   Asia   Antarctica   Australia
Europe   North America   South America   Atlantic Ocean
Pacific Ocean   Indian Ocean   Southern Ocean   Arctic Ocean

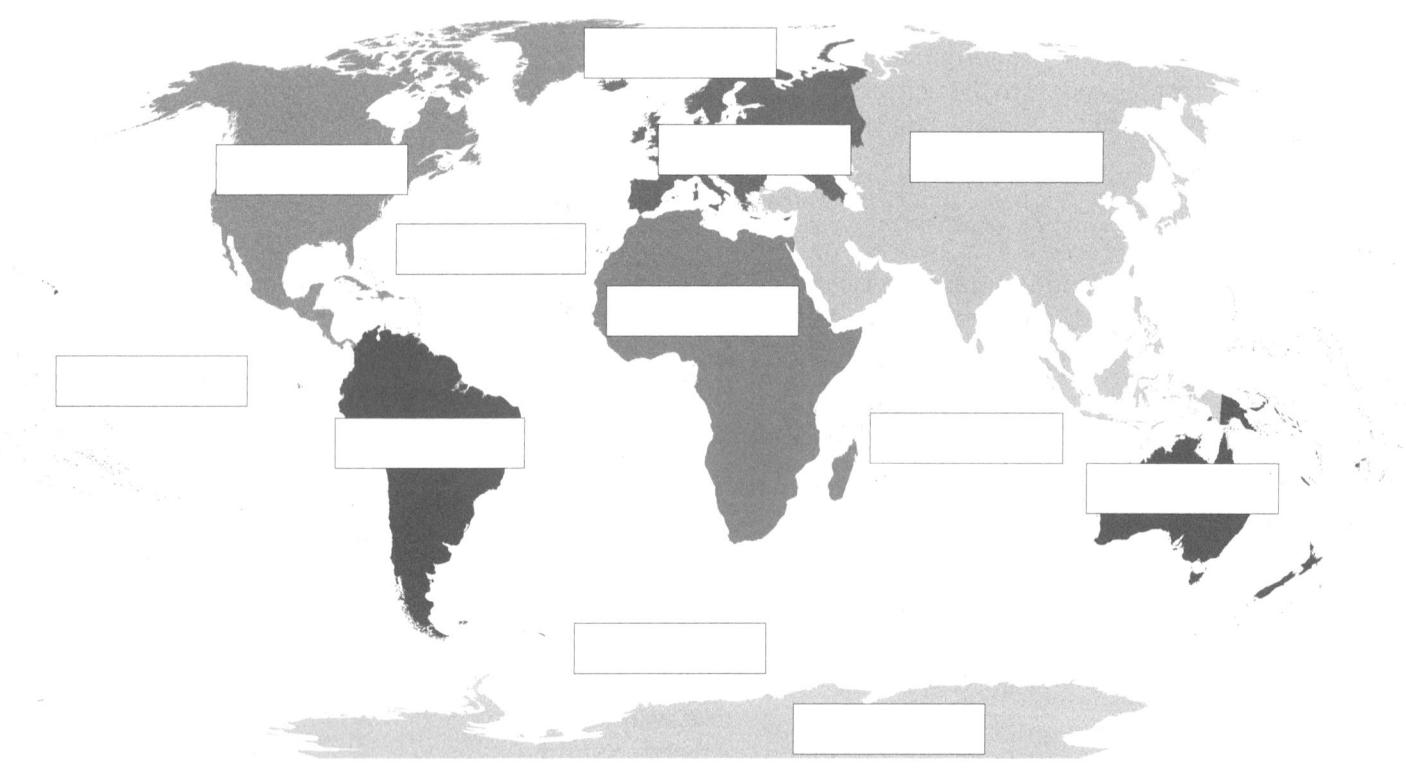

CHAPTER 1
Assessment

2. Write the letter next to the part it shows on the globe.

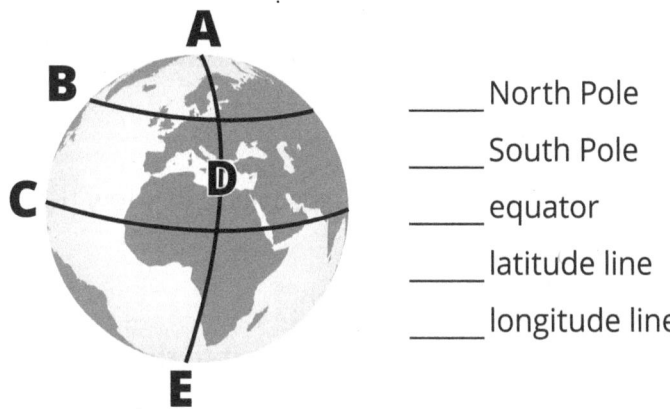

_____ North Pole
_____ South Pole
_____ equator
_____ latitude line
_____ longitude line

3. Label the compass roses to show the cardinal directions.

A.

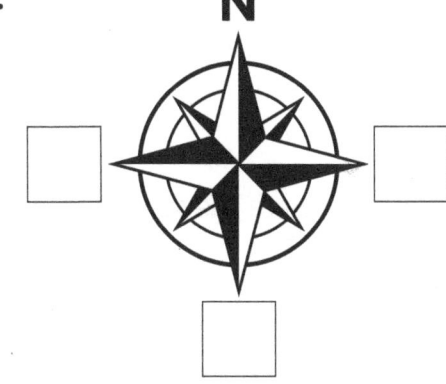

B.

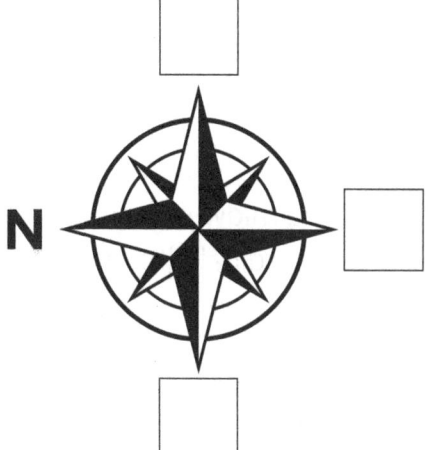

Circle the correct answer to each question.

4. What is a region?

   A. a line that connects the North and South Poles

   B. a round model of Earth

   C. an area of land that has common features or characteristics

5. What are some ways people can divide Earth into regions? Circle all correct answers.

   A. by location

   B. by climate

   C. by culture, such as religion or languages

CHAPTER 1
Assessment

Read each sentence. Circle True or False.

6. True or False   It is important to know your location in the world so you can find places you want or need to go.

7. True or False   A hill is taller than a mountain.

8. True or False   A valley is usually found between two mountains.

9. True or False   Globes are round models of Earth while maps are flat models that can show the whole Earth or part of it.

10. True or False   Oceans, lakes, and rivers are all types of land found on Earth.

11. Put a P next to the items that are physical features found in nature. Put an H next to the items that are human features.

_____ bridge

_____ mountain

_____ house

_____ river

_____ ocean

12. Use the map of the midwest region of the United States to help you complete the sentences below. Circle the correct cardinal direction.

A. Washington (WA) is **north / east** of Oregon (OR).

B. Wyoming (WY) is **west / south** of Montana (MT).

C. Nevada (NV) is **east / south** of California (CA).

D. Utah (UT) is **east / west** of Colorado (CO).

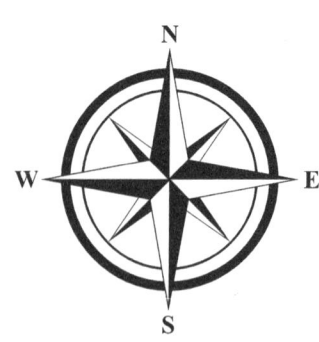

CHAPTER 1
Assessment

Alternative Assessment Answer Key

1.

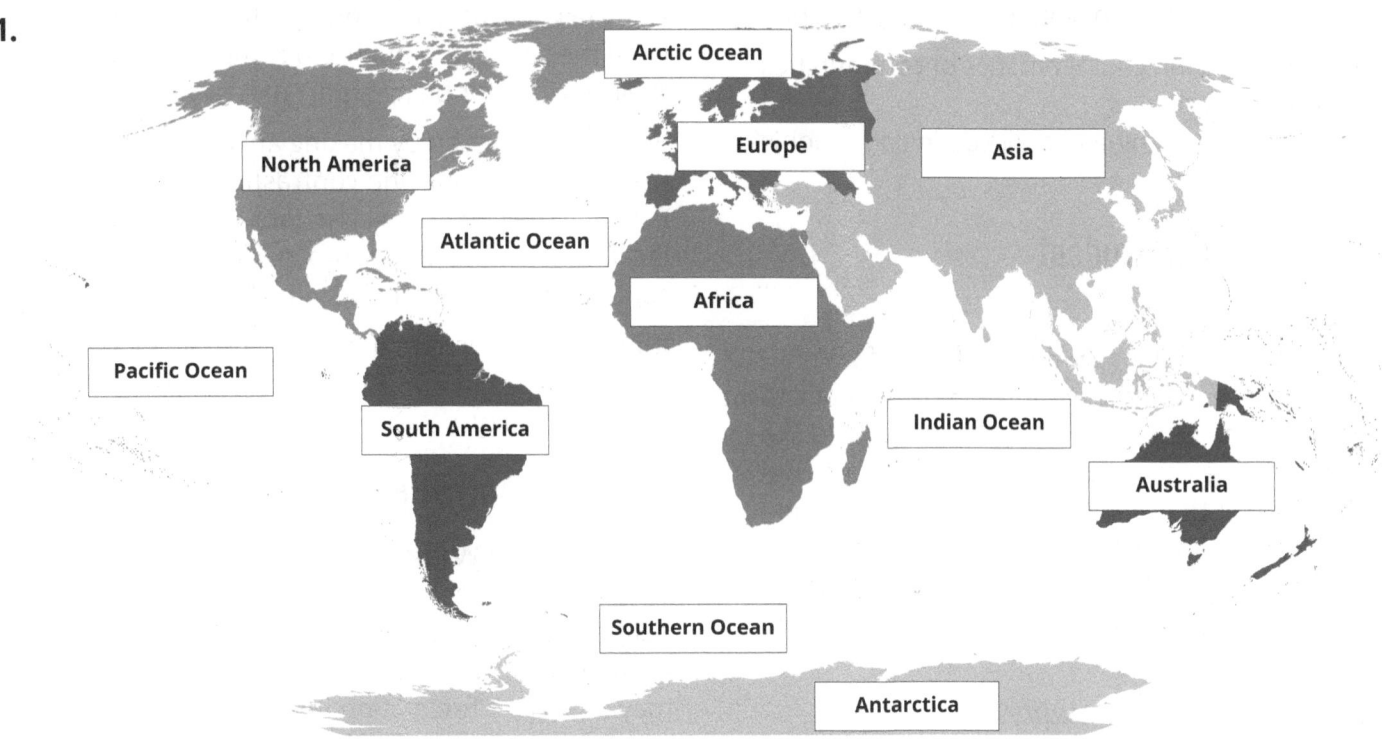

2. A: North Pole
   E: South Pole
   C: equator
   B: latitude line
   D: longitude line

3. A.

   B.

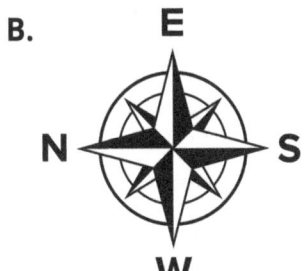

4. C
5. A, B, C
6. True
7. False
8. True
9. True
10. False
11. H: bridge
    P: mountain
    H: house
    P: river
    P: ocean
12. A. north
    B. south
    C. east
    D. west

Discover! SOCIAL STUDIES • GRADE 2 • CHAPTER 1 ASSESSMENT

LESSON 10
Communities Around the World

Lesson Objectives

By the end of this lesson, your student will be able to:

- describe common characteristics of communities around the world
- identify common things people do in communities around the world

Supporting Your Student

Explore
Your student may struggle with thinking of their dream, or ideal, group. Encourage them to brainstorm ideas about their interests or a goal they would like to accomplish. They can build their dream group from that idea. Then they can brainstorm about people in their lives who they think can help. They also may want to add in people they don't know personally but who they think can help their dream group achieve its goal.

Read *(What Is a Community?)*
Help your student identify what members of a community may have in common by prompting them to look at a personal example. They can be prompted to explain how they engage with a community they are a part of and to name what they have in common with the other members. For example, if your student plays at the park with the same group of kids every week, they can identify something that is the same about what they do or how they feel when playing at the park. By relating the concept to personal experience, your student is better able to connect to the content.

Practice
Your student may be overwhelmed when trying to name two of their communities. Support them by helping them make a list or draw pictures of their communities. You may need to ask questions to lead them to some ideas, such as "What do you practice every Thursday at 4:00?" or "Where do we go on Sunday mornings?" Questions like these may help your student recognize their own communities.

Learning Styles

Auditory learners may enjoy interviewing two people from the same community to compare and contrast their reasons for being a part of that community.

Visual learners enjoy making an illustrated Venn diagram comparing and contrasting two communities to which they belong. Assist your student with locating or taking photographs of these different communities to add to the Venn diagram.

Kinesthetic learners may enjoy using blocks, toy building bricks, or empty containers to build a model of a community.

Extension Activities

Community Walk
Take your student on a walk around their neighborhood (or another area) and have them name examples of communities they see. For example, they may observe a fire station nearby with firefighters outside or kids at baseball practice. Challenge your student to find five examples of a community on their walk. If this is not possible, have your student draw, print pictures, or cut pictures out of a magazine to show real-world examples of communities.

Community Riddles
Ask your student to come up with three clues describing a community they know. They should give the clues first while you guess. Then, change roles and give three clues to your student so they can make inferences and guess the community from the clues. Be prepared with extra clues in case they need more support to figure out the answer.

LESSON 10
Communities Around the World

Answer Key

Explore
Answers will vary.

Write *(In what ways are communities all over the world the same?)*
Answers will vary. Possible answers: In all communities, people live and work together. The goal of any community is to help each other live as well as they can. Communities work together to reach a goal. Communities are groups of people with common interests.

Practice
Answers will vary depending on the communities your student is a part of.

Show What You Know
1. Community (circle around them): Any picture with two or more people in it. Not a community (crossed out): Any picture with just one person in it.
2. Answers may vary. Possible answers: They show two people who live or work together. They show a group of people doing a shared activity.
3. A, C, D
4. Answers may vary. Possible answers: play together, have picnics, help each other, have parties, talk, play games, work together

LESSON 11
What Makes Communities Special

Lesson Objectives

By the end of this lesson, you will be able to:
- explain ways that communities can be different from one another
- describe what your community is like
- describe what you like about your community

Supporting Your Student

Create
Your student may struggle with thinking of a superpower that can help their community. Have them think of a problem they want to solve in the community. Then, brainstorm types of superpowers (i.e., x-ray vision or super strength) and assist them in matching one to a problem they have identified in their community.

Read *(The Community Where You Live)*
While reading the information in this section, discuss specific information about your community with your student. Point out different locations specific to your community, such as important landmarks or buildings. It may help to have a map or pictures of your community available for your student to look at. Share what you think makes your community special as an example. Your student may research your community online to look for interesting facts about or people in your community.

Write *(Make a list of special places in your community).*
Your student may need help to name places in their community. If possible, take a walk in your community to point out important buildings or locations. If not possible, support your student by brainstorming ideas with them to help them make their list.

Learning Styles

Auditory learners may enjoy making a pre-planned phone call to a community member you may know who can give them more information about their community.

Visual learners may enjoy making a "Top 5 Reasons We Love _____ (their community)" poster.

Kinesthetic learners may enjoy a short scavenger hunt with you in their community where they travel with you and find special places in the community like a community, church, or library.

Extension Activities

The Superhero Is You!
Challenge your student to create a three-panel comic starring themselves as the superhero they created in the Create activity on the second page of the lesson. They need to show themselves solving the community problem using their superpower.

Standing Together
Have your student research various community groups in your area. Ask them to create a list of the community groups and put a heart next to the groups they may be interested in joining. For example, your student may want to volunteer at the animal shelter or be a part of the community choir. If appropriate, assist them in volunteering for an activity in that group.

LESSON 11
What Makes Communities Special

Answer Key

Explore
Answers will vary. Possible answers: They are the same because people live in them and they have buildings.

They are different because Community 1 has tall buildings and Community 2 does not; Community 2 has a farm and Community 1 does not.

Write *(What is one way communities can be different?)*
Answers will vary. Possible answers: different sizes, locations, interests, populations, space between buildings

Write *(Make a list of special places in your community.)*
Answers will vary. Possible answers: hospital, library, community center, churches

Practice
Drawings will vary. Check that your student drew important places (i.e., library, community center) and drew one person doing their job.

Answers will vary. Possible answers: My community is special because we have a lot of farms that grow food for other communities. My community is special because every spring we have a special pet parade that people go to with their pets.

Show What You Know
1. False
2. True
3. False
4. True
5. Answers may vary. Possible answers:

What size is your community? Is it big or small?	a small/medium/large community
What does your community look like?	a lot of tall buildings or no tall buildings, a lot of people or only a few people, farms, parks
Name two special places in your community.	hospitals, churches, community center, town hall
Name two roles or jobs people have in your community.	doctor, construction worker, farmer, banker, police officer

6. Answers will vary. Possible answers: community groups, the way we take care of each other, our library or museum, our sports teams, our parks, the people in it

LESSON 12
Community Types

Lesson Objectives

By the end of this lesson, your student will be able to:

- describe the differences between urban, suburban, and rural communities
- identify the type of community in which you live

Supporting Your Student

Explore
Your student may need support to choose the community that most resembles theirs because they may feel that none of the pictures match their community well. Discuss with them some similarities that they can find with their own community and at least one picture. Help them understand that while their community may not look exactly like one of those pictures, it most likely has some common qualities with at least one picture.

Practice (Urban, Suburban, or Rural?)
Your student may need support in deciding which community each description is referring to. Help them review the details about each type of community in the Read sections. Remind your student that they can often tell the type of community by looking at how the area is laid out. Houses and buildings in urban communities are usually closer together, while those in rural communities are farther apart.

It may be also important to note for your student that communities gradually expand out from a city center. For example the middle of a big city may be very crowded. The farther you move from the center, the more spread out things get until the communities look like the suburbs. As you move even farther out, you may start to see communities that have even more open space and resemble rural communities.

Practice (My Community)
Your student may become overwhelmed when making a decision about the type of community in which they live. Review the definitions of urban, suburban, and rural with them. Ask them questions to prompt them to compare and contrast the three types of communities with their own community, such as, "How far apart are the homes in your community?," "Are there many tall buildings in your community?," and "Can you walk to a store, or is it a short or long drive to a store in your community?"

Learning Styles

Auditory learners may enjoy making up a song that explains the type of community they live.

Visual learners may enjoy folding a piece of paper into three columns and making a table that lists the characteristics of each type of community. They may choose to draw a picture of each type of community in the corresponding column.

Kinesthetic learners may enjoy playing charades and acting out each type of community for another player to guess. Have them take turns so that your student gets a chance to guess and use their inference skills.

Extension Activities

From Community to World
Have your student research ways that the type of community in which they live contributes to the world in general. For example, a rural community may contribute to the world by growing crops which become the food we eat. Have them make a poster to show what they have learned.

Going on a Trip
Have your student plan an imaginary trip to a different type of community from the one in which they live. For example, if they live in a suburban community, have them plan a trip to an urban community. Have them choose a specific city or town and plan an itinerary for what they will do while they are there. Discuss the differences between activities in the destination community and their own community as they plan.

LESSON 12
Community Types

Answer Key

Explore
Answers will vary depending on your student's community.

Write *(How are urban and suburban communities the same? How are they different?)*
Answers may vary. Possible answers:

(Same) They both have many houses. They both have many stores and restaurants. They both have neighbors that are nearby.

(Different) In an urban community, you can walk to many stores and restaurants; however, in a suburban community, you usually have to drive. In suburban communities, many houses have a backyard where children may play; however, many houses in urban communities have small or no backyards. In an urban community, many people may live in apartments; however, in suburban communities, most people live in houses.

Practice *(Urban, Suburban, or Rural?)*
C: urban community

B: suburban community

A: rural community

Practice *(My Community)*
Answers may vary depending on where your student lives.

Show What You Know
1. rural
2. urban
3. suburban

Discover! SOCIAL STUDIES • GRADE 2 • LESSON 2

LESSON 13
Community Maps

Lesson Objectives

By the end of this lesson, your student will be able to:
- identify common locations found in communities around the world
- use picture symbols to find places on a map of a community

Supporting Your Student

Read *(Places in a Community)*
As your student reads about common locations in communities, reference the locations from the worktext that are found in your community. Consider having your student use a community map to find the location of each place. Additionally, point out that a common location may look different in various communities around the world. For example, a library in some areas may be a huge building where people check out books, use computers, and participate in events like a summer reading program. In other areas, a library might not be a stationary place. It could be a bus or van that someone drives from village to village for people to borrow books to read.

Write *(Why do you think a person reading would be a symbol for a library? Is this a good symbol to use for a library? Why or why not?)*
One way to help your student understand why the symbol of a person reading represents a library is to act it out for them by sitting with an open book. Help them make the connection that the symbol shows a common action in that location (reading). If your student is unfamiliar with the concept of libraries, help them to search online for the history of libraries to help them understand what libraries are and why they were created. You might also search for free online libraries for children so that they can experience a virtual library and appreciate why so many communities have libraries.

Practice
Your student might need your help in understanding some of the symbols on the map. Asking them questions to get them thinking about the types of things that they see in certain locations might be useful. For example, you might ask, "If someone goes to the airport, what might they see?" You can then relate the airplane symbol to the airport because airplanes are commonly seen at airports.

Learning Styles

Auditory learners may enjoy creating a visual map after listening to their instructor's oral description of a community.

Visual learners may enjoy creating their own symbols to represent different rooms in their home, such as the kitchen or home office. Have them discuss their reasoning for choosing each symbol with you.

Kinesthetic learners may enjoy creating a 3D map of their community with differently shaped toy building blocks.

Extension Activities

Mapping It Out
Give your student a small item, such as a coffee mug or a small toy, and have them hide it in another room. Then, have them draw a treasure map with pictures that shows the way to the item. Use the map to find the item. This activity could also be done with a family member or one of your student's siblings or friends.

It's Symbolic
Help your student use an online search engine to research a community different from theirs. Encourage your student to find at least three locations that exist in the researched community that do not exist in their community. Then, challenge your student to create symbols for these new locations and explain the symbols to you.

LESSON 13
Community Maps

Answer Key

Explore

library

hospital

store or market

Write *(Which of the above locations do you have in your community?)*
Answers will vary depending on your student's community.

Write *(Why do you think a person reading would be a symbol for a library? Is this a good symbol to use for a library? Why or why not?)*
Answers will vary. Possible answer: A person reading a book is a good symbol for a library because many people go to the library to borrow books, people may enjoy reading while at the library, and there is story time at the library because the librarian reads books to you.

Practice

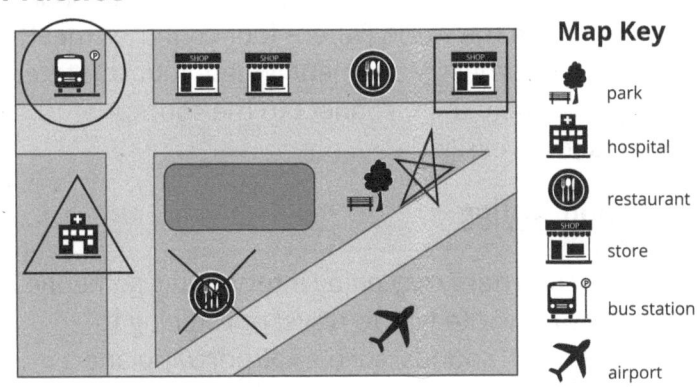

Show What You Know
1. C
2. B
3. A
4. D
5. Possible answers include: hospital, restaurant, store, market, library, park, airport, train station, bus station

LESSON 14
Maps and Travel

Lesson Objectives

By the end of this lesson, your student will be able to:

- use a map key to find locations on a map
- identify symbols on a map for ways people travel in a community
- locate boundaries or borders on a map

Supporting Your Student

Explore
Remind your student that a trip can be anywhere that you go, whether it is short or long. Help them remember all of the different types of trips that they have been on, such as trips to visit family members and friends or trips to vacation spots. Ask them to list all of the different types of transportation that they have used, including cars, buses, trains, and planes. Finally, to help them decide where they would like to go if they could go anywhere in the world, you might ask them what type of weather they would prefer and what they would like to be able to do on their trip. Knowing the answers to those questions could enable you to help them to narrow down some different places that they might like to travel to.

Read *(Travel on a Map)*
To get your student used to interpreting different symbols, you might use a search engine to find different types of emojis, such as the smiley face emoji, the scowling emoji, and the laughing emoji. Ask your student to look at each one carefully to interpret what it means and have them explain how they know whether the emoji is happy, unhappy, etc. You might also help them to do an online search for the labels or logos of different products to see what types of pictures are included in order to indicate something about the product itself. For example, a food product that includes honey might have a picture of a bee on it to show that the honey is pure and natural, or a running shoe might have an animal that is known for its strength or speed as its logo to show that their product is durable. Relate this to how a symbol used for a travel location may show something about the location, such as an airplane showing an airport.

Read *(Borders on a Map)*
One way to help your student connect with the concept of boundaries, especially imaginary boundaries, is to have them look at or think about a doorway between two different rooms, such as a kitchen and a living room. Have them think about how the doorway separates these two rooms and indicates where one room ends and the next begins. Then, if possible, take them on a walk or a drive to explore some of the different boundaries in your community to help them understand how boundaries can be made of real, tangible objects and how they can be invisible or imaginary.

To help them understand what a border is, look up a map of your community so that they can see where one town or city begins and another ends. Help them understand that each town or community has specific borders and that there is a specific governing body that is responsible for the area within those borders. If possible, drive them across the border between two towns or communities to give them a visual representation of an imaginary border.

Finally, searching online for international tripoints (where three countries meet), the only international quadripoint in the world (where four countries meet), or the Four Corners Monument (where four US states meet) could help them connect to the concept of borders more easily.

Learning Styles

Auditory learners may enjoy interviewing someone about their favorite way to travel or listening to different travel sounds, such as airport/airplane sounds, train sounds, etc., that can be found by using a search engine.

Visual learners may enjoy making a map of where they live with clearly marked borders. Your student might choose to draw a map of part of the inside area (marking the borders between some of the rooms and/or other sections) or the outside area (marking the property lines or the borders between other areas on the property).

Kinesthetic learners may enjoy pretending that they

LESSON 14
Maps and Travel

are going on a trip to visit some family members and acting out which method of transportation they would like to use.

Extension Activities

Create a Map Key
Have your student create a simple map of their community and place pictures or symbols of at least three of their favorite places on it. Then have them create a map key to help others read and understand their map.

Know Your Borders
Using a search engine, help your student to find a map of their country and to explore all of the borders. For example, someone who lives in the United States would look at the borders of the entire country before looking at the borders of their individual state, county, city, town, etc. Showing your student all of the different borders that they are in could help them understand this concept better.

Answer Key

Explore
Drawings will vary.

Write *(Which way would you like to travel: airplane, bus, train, or ship? Why?)*
Answers will vary. Possible answer: I would like to travel on an airplane to see what the world looks like from high above.

Practice
Maps will vary. Maps should have clearly drawn borders and three map symbols with their meanings in the map key.

Show What You Know
1. B
2. A
3. B
4. A

LESSON 15
Volunteering in a Community

Lesson Objectives

By the end of this lesson, your student will be able to:
- describe why volunteering is important in a community
- identify ways you can help others in a community

Supporting Your Student

Explore
Guide your student to think about any way that they have helped someone. Sometimes a young child has a hard time understanding that even the smallest acts can be helpful. To clarify this misconception, help them identify the wide range of ways someone can help others. Saying a kind word to someone who is upset, holding the door for someone bringing in packages, or something more overt like helping to wash a car or raking leaves are all ways to help.

Read
As your student reads about volunteering, help them to see how a community may be different without volunteers. If volunteers did not help pick up the litter in the park, it would make it unsafe for people to play. If people did not volunteer to be coaches for sports teams and clubs, children would not have these activities. By volunteering, these community volunteers help make their community a better place to live, work, and play.

Practice
Encourage your student to select a volunteer opportunity that they have an interest in or that is readily available in their area. For example, if your student likes to read, they could volunteer to help organize materials at the library. They could clean up toys in the children's book area or stock bookmarks at the counter.

Learning Styles

Auditory learners may enjoy talking with active volunteers to learn more about the value of being a volunteer.

Visual learners may enjoy showing the positive effects of volunteering in a visual way. Have them fold a piece of paper in half and label the left side "Before" and the right side "After." On the left side of the paper, have them draw someone or a situation in need of a volunteer. On the right side, have them draw themselves assisting in the situation and how it improved.

Kinesthetic learners may enjoy choosing to do the volunteer activity they identified in the Practice section.

Extension Activities

Anywhere Is a Good Place to Volunteer
Have your student choose a place they would like to visit. Help them use the internet to find out how they could volunteer if they lived in that community instead of their own. Then have your student compare the ways people volunteer in that community to their own community. For example, you may have a beach cleanup where you live. In areas not close to the ocean, they may have a community rodeo to raise money for a new community center.

Getting to Know a Volunteer
Contact a community volunteer who is willing to speak with your student. Have your student interview them about their volunteer experience including how and why they started, how volunteering helps the community, and what they like most about it. Have your student make a poster showing what they have learned.

LESSON 15
Volunteering in a Community

Answer Key

Explore
Drawings will vary.

Write *(Why is being a volunteer in your community important?)*
Answers may vary. Possible answer: It helps to make your community a better place.

Practice
Drawings may vary. Possible answers: I can be a community volunteer by helping clean up the park, holding a food drive, or helping my neighbor carry in groceries. This helps my community by keeping the park clean and safe, giving food to people who need it, or getting my neighbor the things they need in a safe way.

Show What You Know
1. D
2. A
3. C
4. B
5. False
6. True
7. True
8. False

LESSON 16
Local Leaders in a Community

Lesson Objectives

By the end of this lesson, your student will be able to:
- explain what local leaders do in a community
- describe what makes a good leader
- identify the leaders in your local government

Supporting Your Student

Read *(Local Leaders in a Community)*
Communities have many different types of leaders. Local leaders can be elected like a mayor or city council. They can also be appointed or hired like the leader of the parks and recreation department or highway administration. As your student reads this section, try to make connections to the types of local leaders you have in your particular area to make the content more meaningful.

Read *(A Good Leader)*
To help your student think about what makes a good leader, guide them to recognize examples of good leaders in their lives. For example, if your student has a coach they like, ask them to identify why they like the coach. Then help them see that those same qualities most likely apply to a good leader. For instance, if your student says they like how the coach teaches them new things, you might mention how leaders often make decisions that allow people to live a better life. They may make decisions to build things like community centers or start new groups in the community for people to learn new skills and hobbies.

Practice
Your student may need support finding the names of their local leaders. Start by checking if there is a city or town hall in your community. If there is not and there is no community website or current newspaper, reach out to another source. A chamber of commerce or a local library may have some information. Also, a community member who has lived in the community for a long time may have some knowledge of either the local leaders' names or where you may get the information.

Learning Styles

Auditory learners may enjoy listening to speeches of past leaders and listing two examples of how that speech showed traits of a good leader.

Visual learners may enjoy making a chart that shows how local government in their community works. For example, the mayor is at the head and consults with and answers to the town council, who consults with and answers to the whole community.

Kinesthetic learners may enjoy taking a walk around their community to identify where the local leaders work or meet. Consider taking a field trip to a local leader's office.

Extension Activities

You Have the Skills
Have your student reread the A Good Leader section and make a list of the traits of a good leader. Have your student identify at least one of those traits that they possess themselves. Challenge them to write or illustrate how they could use this good leadership trait to help the community.

Knowledge Is Power
Have your student make a list of future community meetings that include local leaders. Encourage them to attend one of these meetings with an adult to observe what happens. If this is not possible, have them draw a picture of what they think would happen at one of these meetings.

LESSON 16
Local Leaders in a Community

Answer Key

Explore
Answers will vary.

Write *(What is one thing good leaders do?)*
Answers may vary. Possible answers: A good leader thinks of everyone in the community, listens to others, asks questions, and makes fair decisions.

Practice
Answers will vary depending on your student's community.

Show What You Know
1. This sentence should be crossed out.
2. This sentence should be circled.
3. This sentence should be circled.
4. This sentence should be circled.
5. A
6. A
7. Answers will vary depending on your local community's leader.

LESSON 17
Our Government

Lesson Objectives

By the end of this lesson, your student will be able to:

- describe the goals of government
- identify different ways a government can help its citizens

Supporting Your Student

Explore
Help your student brainstorm the different communities they belong to before they begin to identify community leaders. Remind your student of activities they are involved in that might assist them in identifying communities. Do they play basketball every week or attend Sunday school? Then you can lead your student in recognizing the leaders of each of these communities. Is there a team captain or coach? Who teaches Sunday school? Your student may struggle in recognizing how leaders work to help the community. Ask leading questions, such as "Does your soccer coach help you learn how to score a goal?" or "Does your scout leader help get people together to clean up a park?"

Read
As your student reads, help them connect examples of government goals to their own community, state, or country. When discussing laws, give an example of a law that your student might be familiar with, such as people not being able to steal things. Discuss how this law protects people and keeps them safe.

When discussing rights, emphasize that rights are things that cannot be taken from a citizen. Different countries have different rights; however, there are many rights that are universal, such as having the right to own property and make decisions for yourself.

Practice
Help your student think of examples of ways a government can keep citizens safe. It may be helpful to revisit the Read sections. Point out specific examples, such as forming groups to help people get food they need. Then discuss ideas for how your student may draw this. For example, they might draw a picture of someone handing a box of food to someone else, much like the picture in the Read section.

Learning Styles

Auditory learners may enjoy pretending they are a leader giving a speech about one way they would help their country.

Visual learners may enjoy making a timeline of three different programs in their country that were started to help its citizens.

Kinesthetic learners may enjoy acting out a government goal or a way governments can help citizens. For example, they might pretend to pass a law or collect food for citizens who need it.

Extension Activities

Writing for Change
Have your student write a letter to a national lawmaker where they live, recommending a new program that would benefit the citizens of their country. You can encourage them to explain at least three reasons why it would benefit the citizens.

Building a Government
Have your student research the location of where laws are made in your town, state, territory, province, or country. They can look at pictures of the building and the rooms where leaders make decisions. Then have your student create a model of the building.

LESSON 17
Our Government

Answer Key

Explore
Drawings and answers will vary.

Write *(What is one way a government can help its citizens?)*
Answers may vary. Possible answers: giving food to people, helping them pay their bills if they lose their job, helping older people get food and medicine, protecting people's right to homeschool, helping pay for buildings and teachers for schools

Practice
Answers may vary. Possible answers:

(Helping citizens) giving food to people, helping older people get to the doctors, building schools, protecting children's right to homeschool

(Keeping citizens safe) giving police and firefighters equipment to help others, making laws

Show What You Know
1. safe
2. laws
3. rights
4. need
5. A, B, D

LESSON 18
A Country's Leader

Lesson Objectives

By the end of this lesson, your student will be able to:
- describe the responsibilities of a country's leaders
- identify ways a country can remember their past leaders

Supporting Your Student

Read
As your student reads the various sections in the lesson, it is important to emphasize that different countries have different expectations for their leader. For example, in some countries, the leader can make their own laws and rules. In other countries, they may only have some power to approve laws. Additionally, some countries' leaders are elected while others are appointed or are given the job because they are born into a certain family. As your student reads, make connections between the information and your own country's leader and their responsibilities.

Read *(Remembering Past Leaders)*
Remind your student that all of the ways people can remember a past leader of the country may also be applied to other leaders as well. For example, there may be other leaders of national importance who have monuments, memorials, or even holidays in your country. On a smaller scale, there might be monuments or memorials in your community that honor local leaders.

Practice
As your student prepares to draw, ask them to think about what actions would show a leader following the responsibilities from the lesson. For example, if they wanted to show a leader listening to the citizens, ask them to describe what they would see that would let them know a leader was listening, such as holding a meeting and asking questions.

Learning Styles

Auditory learners may enjoy describing what they think would make a good leader of a country.

Visual learners may enjoy looking up images of currencies or monuments from different countries that honor important leaders.

Kinesthetic learners may enjoy playing "Responsibility Charades." Have your student act out different responsibilities while you guess which responsibility they are miming.

Extension Activities

Biography of a Leader
Have your student research a current or past leader of your country. They should find their birthdate, birthplace, date of death, and place of death, if applicable. Have your student list three ways the leader helped your country. Your student can present their findings in an oral report on what they have learned.

It's an Honor
Have your student research the history of a monument or memorial in a country they would like to visit. Make sure they include the person of honor, reason they are honored, date the monument was built, and whether someone can visit that monument today. Have them include at least one picture. Your student can then make a poster to present what they have learned.

LESSON 18
A Country's Leader

Answer Key

Explore
Drawings will vary.

Write *(What is one responsibility a country's leader has?)*
Answers may vary. Possible answers: A country's leader should keep citizens safe. They can help approve or make laws and rules, listen to citizens' concerns, motivate citizens to make the country a better place, and work with other leaders around the country and world to solve problems.

Practice
Drawings will vary.

Show What You Know
1. B
2. A
3. C
4. True
5. False
6. True
7. False

LESSON 19
Laws

Lesson Objectives

By the end of this lesson, your student will be able to:

- describe why governments make laws
- identify why laws are important in the community and country
- identify laws that keep people and places in the community safe
- recognize the difference between fair and unfair laws

Supporting Your Student

Explore
Your student may need support thinking about what happens when they do not follow a rule. For example, if they draw themselves brushing their teeth on the left, they could draw themselves having to get cavities filled if they do not follow it on the right. Assist them in understanding how doing the action stated in the rule does help them improve their lives. You can ask, "How does doing _____ help to make your life better? What does it do that is good for you?"

Read
Your student may need help understanding how laws keep them safe. Ask them questions such as, "What would happen if everyone was allowed to hit each other?" or "Would you feel safe walking across the street if everyone could drive as fast as they wanted?"

Practice
Your student may need support understanding the concept of fair and unfair. As an example, ask them if they think the first statement is fair. If they say yes, ask them how they would feel if they lived in a yellow house in that community. Then they would not get to vote for the president.

Acknowledge that in the past and even today there are unfair laws. For example, in some countries people could not own property, live freely, or vote because of their skin color or religious beliefs. This meant other groups were favored and could do things these groups could not.

Learning Styles

Auditory learners may enjoy listening to a speech made by someone who fought to end unfair laws globally or, if possible, in their local community.

Visual learners may enjoy making a poster showing a law in their community and why it is important.

Kinesthetic learners may enjoy taking a walk around their community and finding three examples of laws being followed.

Extension Activities

Opposite Land
Have your student design a three- to five-panel comic to show a world where the laws are the opposite of what they usually are. For example, someone would break a law if they tried to pay for something in a store or if they stopped at a red light. Have a discussion with your student to help them understand through this exercise why laws are important. Have them present this comic to others and let your student explain it.

That's Not Fair
Have your student identify a law in their community or another community that they believe is unfair. Have them make a poster naming the law, telling why they think it is unfair, and how they believe the law should change. Your student can then do an oral report to present what they have learned.

LESSON 19
Laws

Answer Key

Explore
Drawings may vary.

Write *(How can you know if a law is fair or unfair?)*
Answers may vary. Possible answers: An unfair law shows favor to a group of people. Fair laws do not favor one group over another.

Practice
1. C
2. A
3. B
4. Unfair
5. Fair
6. Fair
7. Unfair

Show What You Know
1. E
2. B
3. A
4. D
5. C
6. A
7. Answers may vary. Possible answers: Everyone can use the public library. People with a birthday in any month can use the public library. The public library is open to any community member.

LESSON 20
Elections and Voting

Lesson Objectives

By the end of this lesson, your student will be able to:
- describe an election process
- identify a way people can vote or have their opinions heard in your country

Supporting Your Student

Explore
Your student may benefit from discussing how a family may make this decision fairly. Give them examples that family members may raise their hands or write down their choices to say what they want, and then an adult may count the choices and find the winner.

Take a Closer Look
One way to support your student is to use guided questions to help them determine whether a statement is true or false. For example, the first statement says, "The candidate should travel to different places and give speeches to explain why they should be elected." You might ask, "How could going to different places and giving speeches that explain the reasons that people should vote for them help a candidate? Why might more people vote for a candidate who does these things?" Questions like those could help your student think about why those things would be beneficial and determine that the statement is true.

Practice
One way to support your student is to begin with the first statement and use guided questions to help your student figure out if the statement is something that would occur early in the election process or toward the end. Doing so could help your student place the statements in the correct order. For example, the first statement is, "Voters cast their vote for the candidate they think is best." If your student is struggling, you might ask, "What kinds of things have to happen before a voter can actually vote?" You might also have your student try to work backward and find the statement that describes what happens last.

Learning Styles

Auditory learners may enjoy creating a radio ad or podcast for a political candidate or helping make a family decision. For example, they might create a podcast that explains why their family should vote for having a picnic in the park for the next family outing instead of going to the zoo.

Visual learners may enjoy creating a poster that encourages people in their community to vote.

Kinesthetic learners may enjoy playing a game of charades and acting out different aspects of the election process, such as a voter casting a ballot, a candidate giving a speech, or a poll worker counting the ballots.

Extension Activities

Vote for Me!
Have your student pretend to be a candidate in an election in your community. Have them write out their goals for improving the community, and a short speech explaining why these goals are important as well as why citizens should vote for them. You might also have your student create a poster that encourages voters to choose them and a campaign slogan to catch voters' interest.

Vote to Be Heard
Have your student choose something that they and a few of their friends may vote on, like movie night, a snack, a short trip, or something that matches the group's needs. Have them prepare ballots and talk to their friends about each choice, and then let the friends vote. Your student should count the votes and announce the winner to their friends.

LESSON 20
Elections and Voting

Answer Key

Write *(What is the difference between an election and an appointment?)*
Answers may vary. Possible answers: An election is when people get to vote for candidates and the person with the most votes wins that government position or office. An appointment is when someone from the government chooses someone for a government position.

Practice

3: Voters cast their vote for the candidate they think is best.

1 (or 2): Voters sign up, or register, to vote.

2 (or 1): Voters learn all about candidates from speeches, ads, and information they read on their own to decide who would be the best leader.

4: The votes are counted and the winner of the election, or the new leader, is announced.

Show What You Know
1. ads
2. ballot
3. Candidates
4. run
5. False
6. True
7. True
8. True
9. Answers will depend on the types of voting options in your student's country.

LESSON 21
Citizens in a Community

Lesson Objectives

By the end of this lesson, your student will be able to:
- explain the meaning of the word *citizen*
- describe how citizens should behave in a community
- identify examples of consequences citizens face when they break a law

Supporting Your Student

Explore
You may need to help your student brainstorm different rules or laws in their community so that they can come up with something to draw. Often, children don't realize that things are laws because they have become habits (like buckling a seatbelt), or they may not know about some laws because they are too young (like speeding). Talk with them about the laws in your community and help them pick one to draw. They may also need help figuring out how to depict a law, such as showing a child in a car with their seatbelt on or throwing litter into a garbage can.

Read *(What Is a Citizen?)*
Talk with your student about your own citizenship and let them know if you are a citizen by birth or if you are a naturalized citizen. You can talk about where your family is from and if their citizenship changed. It is helpful for your student to get multiple examples of what a citizen is.

Read *(Laws in a Community)*
Try to take your time in these sections and talk about each of the different laws individually after reading the information. Understanding laws can be difficult for children, and it can be helpful if they learn why a law was made. Maybe it is for safety or for protecting the environment. Explain to your student that there is a scale of severity depending on the law being broken. You do not want your student to think they will be sent to jail if they accidentally drop a wrapper one time and do not notice. You could give examples of smaller crimes (like littering) and the consequences that go along with them. It is also helpful to relate them to things that they experience regularly, like there is a more severe consequence when they hit a sibling than there is for simply forgetting to do a chore.

Learning Styles

Auditory learners may enjoy listening to a reading of a book about citizenship. Some great books are *Citizenship: Being a Good Citizen* by Adrian Vigliano and *Being a Good Citizen* by Mary Small.

Visual learners may enjoy making drawings of people being good citizens.

Kinesthetic learners may enjoy getting out there and exploring their neighborhood and seeing the different things they get to do as a citizen of their community. You can ask them questions about different situations they may run into when it comes to laws and community expectations.

Extension Activities

Citizenship: Interview
If you or someone you know has gone through the process of becoming a naturalized citizen of a country, see if they would be willing to sit down with your student for an interview. Make sure your student prepares for the interview by writing down the questions that they want to ask. Encourage your student to ask the person about the steps they have had to follow to become a citizen of the country.

Being a Good Citizen
Set up and role-play different situations where your student can show how to be a good citizen. Some situations you could act out are:

1. Waiting patiently in line for a turn at an activity (like waiting at a grocery store or waiting to order food).
2. What your student should do if they find litter. Talk about ways to pick it up safely, or what kinds of litter they should leave alone (like broken glass).
3. Accidentally sending a toy or ball over a neighbor's fence. What should they do to get it back? (They should have an adult knock on the door and ask to get it back.)

LESSON 21
Citizens in a Community

You and your student can come up with many other situations that may be more specific to the area where you live. Have fun acting these scenes out and discuss any questions your student may have.

Answer Key

Explore
Drawings may vary. Possible answers: person wearing a seatbelt, picking up trash, waiting patiently in line

Write *(What community or communities are you a citizen of?)*
Answers may vary depending on the country or community your student is a part of.

Write *(What are some rules of your home? What are the consequences of breaking the rules?)*
Answers may vary. Your student should write down one household rule and the consequence that occurs for breaking that rule.

Practice
Answers may vary. Possible answers:
4. Pay a fine
5. Not allowed to go back to the place
6. Fix what is broken

Show What You Know
7. B
8. C
9. A
10. B
11. A, B, C
12. D

LESSON 22
Chapter 2 Review

Lesson Objectives

By the end of this lesson, your student will review the following big ideas from Chapter 2.

- Communities have similarities and differences. (Lesson 12)
- People can use community maps to find landmarks, streets, and other things. (Lesson 13)
- Volunteering helps our communities. (Lesson 15)
- Different types of governments, leaders, and laws exist in our communities and country. (Lesson 16 and Lesson 17)
- Citizens can vote and participate in the electoral process. (Lesson 20)

Supporting Your Student

Review *(Communities)*
Work with your student to differentiate between the work that a volunteer does and the work that someone does at their job where they get paid. One is paid and the other is not. A volunteer job is usually done to help another person. A paying job may or may not be helping others. Have your student think of some examples of jobs that volunteers do in your community and similar jobs that paid employees do.

Practice *(Vocabulary Story)*
With the fill-in-the-blank story, you can help your student with the words. Discuss the meaning of each word before reading the story. Have your student read each sentence and think of a word from the word box that best fits into the sentence.

Practice *(Concept Sort)*
With your student, discuss what laws are, the consequences of breaking those laws, and parts of the election process. Before reading the phrases, have your student think of a common law and what might happen as a consequence of breaking that law. Then discuss what you do when you vote.

Learning Styles

Auditory learners may enjoy listening to interviews of community leaders on television to see what they have been doing in your community or another community.

Visual learners may enjoy watching a documentary about volunteering in your community.

Kinesthetic learners may enjoy creating a skit about the election process and then acting it out.

Extension Activities

Community Type Collage
Help your student find pictures of your community and local leaders. Have them cut them out and make a collage of the pictures. Then have them research laws in your community with your help. See what laws and rules these leaders created and supported for your community.

Gameboard
Have your student create a game board about their own community. Include places from their community on the gameboard. Include dice. Have your student create a community map based on the information from the gameboard. Then use the community map to find different areas around their community. Make sure they create a map key.

Answer Key

Practice *(Vocabulary Story)*

LESSON 22
Chapter 2 Review

Mary lives in a small <u>community</u>. She wants to <u>improve</u> the community, or make a better area in her neighborhood. She and her <u>neighbor</u>, who lives next door, will pick up trash. They will <u>volunteer</u> because they don't want to get paid for it. Mary looks at a <u>community map</u> to find a good location. The <u>map key</u> on the map shows a thick line. The line is a <u>symbol</u> on the map. It means that there is a highway near the edge of the town. They will go there to start picking up trash.

Practice *(Crossword Puzzle)*

Across:

3. rights

4. citizen

6. appointed

7. laws

Down:

1. police

2. motivate

5. military

Practice *(Concept Sort)*
1. C
2. A
3. B
4. A
5. A
6. B
7. C
8. B
9. C

CHAPTER 2
Assessment

Quick Review

Refer to the statement your student circled in the Show What You Know section to self-assess their knowledge of the chapter concepts. Then to assist in determining if your student is ready to take the assessment, consider:

- Having your student find symbols on a community map and ask questions about what those symbols mean.
- Having your student discuss the responsibilities of local leaders and citizens in communities.

CHAPTER 2
Assessment

Chapter Assessment

Project: Community Poster

Project Requirements or Steps:

Research about your community, your community's laws, and your community's leaders. Look for what makes your community unique or different from other communities.

1. Research online or use other resources to find information about your community, such as:

    a. Are there parks, festivals, races, or other fun things to do in your community?

    b. What laws make your community safe?

    c. Look at information about your community's leaders. Were these leaders elected? When were they elected?

2. Create a poster of the information that you found. Make sure that it has printed or drawn pictures for each part (community, leaders, laws) and include the information for each part.

CHAPTER 2
Assessment

Chapter Assessment Rubric

Use the following rubric to grade your student's assessment.

	4	3	2	1	Points
Connection to the Chapter	The infographic is clearly connected to the chapter.	The infographic is connected to the chapter.	The infographic is somewhat connected to the chapter.	The infographic is not related to the chapter.	
Creativity	The infographic is very creative and aesthetically appealing.	The infographic is creative and aesthetically appealing.	The infographic is somewhat creative and aesthetically appealing.	The infographic is not creative or aesthetically appealing.	
Poster	The information or data is very accurate and easy to follow.	The information or data is accurate.	The information or data is somewhat accurate.	The information or data is not accurate.	
Grammar and Mechanics	There are no grammar or punctuation mistakes.	There are one or two grammar or punctuation mistakes.	There are several grammar or punctuation mistakes.	There are a distracting number of grammar or punctuation mistakes.	

Total Points _____/16

Average _____

CHAPTER 2
Assessment

Alternative Assessment

It is recommended that the instructor provides the student with support during the assessment to include reading and explaining directions, reading any unknown words or phrases, allowing the student to provide verbal responses that are then recorded, and allowing the student to complete sections of the assessment over the course of the day(s).

Read each sentence. Circle True or False.

1. True or False   People live and work together in a community.
2. True or False   In a community, many people can have parties or picnics.
3. True or False   Communities can only be big and not small.
4. True or False   Some communities have parks.
5. True or False   Most communities have libraries, hospitals, restaurants, and parks.
6. True or False   Local leaders in a community break the laws.
7. True or False   A good leader makes decisions without listening to the citizens.
8. True or False   A local leader in the government is a mayor.
9. True or False   The government might pay for the police and military.
10. True or False   A country's leaders must pay its citizens money.
11. True or False   Governments make laws to keep its citizens safe.
12. True or False   One type of law is the traffic law.
13. True or False   People who break the law could have to go to a job to work.

Match the word with its meaning.

14. ____ urban community
15. ____ suburban community
16. ____ rural community
17. ____ monument
18. ____ memorial
19. ____ citizen

A. a building or statue that honors something or someone from the past

B. a person who is part of a larger community

C. a ceremony or other way to honor someone

D. a community outside a city where houses are close together but with some space in-between them

E. a community that usually has some farmland and fewer people

F. a community that has many tall buildings and houses that are close to each other.

Discover! SOCIAL STUDIES • GRADE 2 • CHAPTER 2 ASSESSMENT   59

CHAPTER 2
Assessment

Use the map to answer questions 20–23. Choose the best answer for each question.

20. Where is the camping park?

A. near the train track

B. near the mountains

C. near the shop

D. far away from a car

21. Where are the mountains on the map?

A. near the shop

B. far away from trees

C. near the farm

D. near the bus

22. How do people travel in this community?

A. trains only

B. trains and cars only

C. trains, cars, and buses

D. airplanes

23. What does the thick, black line mean?

A. a big highway

B. the border of the community

C. a road

D. a railroad track

CHAPTER 2
Assessment

Choose the best answer for each question.

24. Why should people volunteer?

A. because it gets people into trouble

B. because it keeps people out of trouble

C. because it makes a community better

D. because people get paid

25. How can you help others in your community?

A. speed in a car

B. pay people

C. pick flowers

D. collect trash

26. How can a government help its citizens?

A. take people to jail

B. provide education for its children

C. make people elect them

D. travel to other countries

27. What is the capital of the United States?

A. Canada

B. Washington, DC

C. Orlando

D. Los Angeles

28. Which of the following would be an unfair law?

A. do not throw trash on the ground

B. keep your hands and feet to yourself

C. people must eat hamburgers on Fridays

D. do not speed in cars

29. How can people have their opinions heard?

A. traveling around

B. posting ads

C. voting

D. obeying the laws

30. What is the election process?

A. People go around and pick up trash.

B. People make decisions for all citizens.

C. People volunteer in a neighborhood.

D. Candidates run in an election for a leader position.

31. How should citizens behave in a community?

A. drive to a job

B. respect each other

C. pay people

D. throw snowballs

CHAPTER 2
Assessment

Alternative Assessment Answer Key

1. True
2. True
3. False
4. True
5. True
6. False
7. False
8. True
9. True
10. False
11. True
12. True
13. False
14. F
15. D
16. E
17. A
18. C
19. B
20. A
21. D
22. C
23. C
24. C
25. D
26. B
27. B
28. C
29. C
30. D
31. B

LESSON 23
What Are Resources?

Lesson Objectives

By the end of this lesson, your student will be able to:
- explain ways people use resources to live, work, and play
- describe how resources can impact how people live, work, and play in a community

Supporting Your Student

Explore
If your student is unsure about any of the jobs shown in the picture, ask guided questions about their clothing or the objects they are holding. For example, you might ask, "Who would need to wear a hard hat at work?" or "Why would someone have to carry a tray for their job? What might be on the tray?" Questions such as these could help your student identify the different types of jobs depicted in the picture.

Read *(What Are Resources?)*
To help your student understand how many resources they use each day, have them describe some things that they do each day. Then ask them questions to help them understand what type(s) of resources they use to do those things. For example, if they say that they brush their teeth each morning, you might ask, "What kind of natural resource do you use to brush your teeth? What kinds of capital resources do you use?" Questions like these can help your student appreciate just how many resources that they use every day.

In the Real World *(Important Jobs in Your Community)*
If your student is having trouble choosing a job that is important to your community, ask them some guided questions. For example, you might ask, "What would we do if no one worked at the grocery store? Where would we get our food?" or "What might happen if no one worked at the auto repair shop? What would we do if we had trouble with our car?" Questions such as these could help your student think about why human resources are important to your community.

Learning Styles

Auditory learners may enjoy recording themselves telling the story of a resource they would like to explore in their community.

Visual learners may enjoy creating a map of their community, drawing various resources that can be found in the community.

Kinesthetic learners may enjoy a neighborhood walk or bike ride where they see various resources in action.

Extension Activities

Resources at Home
Ask your student to think of some natural, human, and capital resources that they have in their home. Have them list as many as possible. Remind your student that when they help out with chores, they are a human resource.

Community Charades
Create a simple game of charades with your student using community resources that have been discussed, such as food, homes, hospitals, and schools.

Answer Key

In the Real World *(Nature vs. Human-Made)*

LESSON 23
What Are Resources?

Answers may vary. Possible answers: Trees and grass are part of nature. Houses, buildings, and cars are made by people.

Explore

Answers may vary. Possible answers: Jobs people have include news reporter, firefighter, doctor, businessperson, police officer, construction worker, and server. Reporters tell people what is going on in a community. Firefighters put out fires and keep people safe. Doctors help people when they are sick. Businesspeople provide different services. Police officers help keep people safe. Builders make homes, buildings, and roads.

Write *(What is the difference between natural and human resources?)*

Answers may vary. Possible answers: Natural resources are found in nature, like water or soil. Human resources are the people who work to make things and provide services that we need.

Write *(What kinds of resources for playing does your community have?)*

Answers may vary. Possible answers: a swimming pool, a park, a playground

Show What You Know

1. True
2. True
3. True
4. True
5. False
6. True
7. Answers may vary. Possible answers: People need water to drink and live well. People can go swimming, boating, or fishing in water.

LESSON 24
Goods and Services

Lesson Objectives

By the end of this lesson, your student will be able to:
- define the words *goods* and *service*
- explain the difference between goods and services
- identify ways businesses and community organizations provide goods and services to people
- describe how new businesses and businesses that close can change a community's economy

Supporting Your Student

Write *(What is a good or service that you or your family has bought or used?)*
If your student is struggling to come up with ideas about which businesses your family visits frequently for goods and services, they may benefit from concrete examples from around the house. Various goods can be pointed to, and services can be referenced with questions such as "Who cuts your hair?"

Practice *(Comparing Goods and Services)*
Your student may struggle with the concept of a Venn diagram. They could benefit from a quick demonstration about how a Venn diagram works. This demonstration can be done by creating a Venn diagram comparing you and them. This assistance provides a tangible example of how to use the Venn diagram before they get started on tackling the lesson content. You can also prompt your student as they complete the diagram by saying something like "Look at the book on our table. Is that a type of good or service? Where would I put it on the diagram?" When they answer, you can have them try again or congratulate them before moving on to the next concept.

Create
Your student may struggle to come up with ideas of goods to sell. Help your student to think of goods that they see in the store or use everyday. Once they have created a list of goods, encourage them choose some goods from their list that they could make or sell. You may also display this process by saying, "I see lots of fruit at the store and in our house. I could make smoothies out of these fruits to sell to others on hot days." Remind your student that they can create new goods that no one else has sold before.

Learning Styles

Auditory learners may enjoy creating a song about goods and services or recording a podcast about a new business that is opening in their community.

Visual learners may enjoy a matching game using images of goods that go with the written name. For example, they could match the word "books" with the picture card of "books." Your student could also draw pictures of goods and services and have their family members guess whether the picture shows goods or services.

Kinesthetic learners may enjoy creating goods that could be sold in a business, such as making lemonade from scratch.

Extension Activities

Exploring Our Neighborhood
Go on a neighborhood scavenger hunt either by driving or walking. Have your student come up with a list of 10 different services they see on the hunt. Bring a paper or notebook along so they can write down their list.

Acting Out a Service
Encourage your student to name a service they know about already and are genuinely interested in learning more about. Then, have your student act out everything they know about that service. For example, if your student chose "flight attendant," you could prompt them with questions about what a flight attendant does and says. Encourage your student to fully engage in the role play. Once the role play is finished, ask your student what they noticed, how they felt, and if they learned anything new about the service they are interested in. In this way, your student can enrich their engagement with the content.

LESSON 24
Goods and Services

Answer Key

Explore
Answers may vary. Possible answers:

1. grocery store; food market
2. chicken, apples, oranges, etc.
3. candy, bananas, carrots, etc.

Write *(What are goods or services that you or your family has bought or used? Why did you need it?)*
Answers will vary. Possible answers: a haircut so my hair isn't long, food that is eaten, toys to play with, clothes to wear

Practice *(Good or Service)*
The soccer ball and the book are goods. Cutting hair is a service.

Write *(What can happen when a new business opens in a community?)*
Answers may vary. Possible answers: Jobs can be created. People get money from working at the jobs and can then spend it on goods and services in the community. The business might provide new goods or services for the community.

Practice *(Comparing Goods and Services)*
Answers may vary. Possible answers include:

(Goods) books, balls, things, video games, food, etc.

(Services) cutting hair, helping people feel better, mowing laws, etc.

(Both) people can pay money for them, people can need or want them, both can be sold at stores

Show What You Know
1. goods
2. economy
3. Services
4. A, C
5. B, C
6. True
7. False
8. True

LESSON 25
Do You Need It? Needs Vs. Wants

Lesson Objectives

By the end of this lesson, your student will be able to:
- describe the difference between needs and wants
- identify how people can get what they want and need

Supporting Your Student

Read *(What Do We Need To Survive?)*
Your student may not be familiar with the concept of survival. They may need additional examples to go along with the reading, such as what would happen if a person didn't have food, water, shelter, or air. Additionally, your student may not think of these items often or of their importance in their everyday lives. Needs tend to be those things that are taken for granted. Your student can gain a greater appreciation for the items in their lives that help them to survive. When needed, prompt your student with questions that target comprehension such as "What are some items that your family gives you that are needed?"

Write *(Imagine that you are stranded on a desert island and have to survive. What are the three most important items you would bring with you? Why did you choose these items?)*
To support your student in coming up with ideas for items to bring on a desert island, you can model the process for them by coming up with your own list and talking it through. For example, you could say, "I would bring food because I don't want to starve." Your example can give them ideas for backing up their thoughts and building on their thinking skills.

Read *(Needs vs. Wants)*
Help your student recall the different ways that people can get what they want and need. Point out that many things we want or need can be acquired in multiple ways. For example, you could build a house yourself or buy one. People can buy food or toys from a store, but they could also grow food and make their own toys. Emphasize that people can also get what they need from nature, including sources of freshwater and materials like wood or stone for building things.

Learning Styles

Auditory learners may enjoy creating their own podcast about needs and wants. Encourage your student to get creative, including sound effects! If possible, have a family member listen to your student's podcast.

Visual learners may enjoy creating drawings to show wants and needs, including creating drawings to show how they might get something they want or need, such as planting seeds in a garden to grow food.

Kinesthetic learners may enjoy playing a game of "Survivor." They can find items around their house that would help them if they are stranded on an island. Once they have gathered their materials, have them describe if they are wants or needs.

Extension Activities

Exploring the Store
Take your student with you to the grocery store to buy the items you need and some you may want. Ask them to help you make a list before you go. As you explore the store, discuss why the items are needs or wants.

Scavenger Hunt
Go on a scavenger hunt around the house. Have your student search for items that are needed. Then, try the activity again, but this time searching for wants.

LESSON 25
Do You Need It? Needs Vs. Wants

Answer Key

Explore
Drawings will vary.

Write
Answers may vary. Possible answers:

1. I would bring <u>food</u> because <u>I don't want to be hungry</u>.
2. I would bring <u>water</u> because <u>I will be thirsty</u>.
3. I would bring <u>a tent</u> because <u>I need shelter</u>.

Practice
Needs: water, healthy food, house, air

Wants: books, toys, video games, TV

Show What You Know
1. B
2. B
3. D
4. True
5. True
6. False
7. Answers may vary. Possible answers: The difference between needs and wants is that a need is something you wouldn't survive without while a want is something you don't need to live but are nice to have.

LESSON 26
Jobs and Income

Lesson Objectives

By the end of this lesson, your student will be able to:
- state the meaning of the word *income*
- explain how a person or family uses income
- explain different choices people can make about what they do for a job

Supporting Your Student

Read *(What Is Income?)*
Support your student in understanding income and how it is used by giving real-world examples. Explain what people in your family do to earn an income. Then, give examples of how your family uses the income. For example, you might say, "Remember when we went to the store and I paid for your book with money? I was using our family's income to buy it."

Read *(Types of Jobs)*
As your student reads this section, encourage them to think about different jobs they see in their community. For example, when they go to the movie theater, who is there to help them? What do they do? There are people whose jobs are to sell tickets, prepare food, and clean the movie theater. Point out that there are often people doing many different jobs in one location.

Practice
Encourage your student to name different jobs. In terms of choosing which one they would like, encourage your student to detail what they know about each job they name. You can further extend their learning by helping them research what each job entails. In this way, your student may be able to deepen their connection to the content and make a more authentic choice about what may interest them.

Learning Styles

Auditory learners may enjoy creating a chant about the value of each piece of currency used in their country, such as "penny, penny, a penny is one cent, one cent." They could then record the chants and listen to them.

Visual learners may enjoy creating a drawing of a workplace, where someone can work. For example, a doctor's office or a toy factory.

Kinesthetic learners may enjoy acting out a dream job. To help your student get the most out of their role play, ask them for details about how the person in their chosen job might act, what they might wear, and what they might say. You can even ask them how a person in their chosen job might feel. Such prompts can help your student make a personal connection to the content.

Extension Activities

Exploring a Business
If possible, take your child to tour a business where people work to make goods and earn an income in your community. Some places to visit could be a working farm, potato chip factory, or bakery.

Using Money
Help your student set up a store. Help them label items with prices and invite their family to shop. Encourage your student to practice the skill of buying and selling things to see using income in action. Prompt them with questions such as "If you don't have enough money, can you buy the goods you want? Why or why not?"

LESSON 26
Jobs and Income

Answer Key

Explore

Answers will vary. Possible answers:

I think this person is <u>delivering mail, shipping boxes, or a driver</u>.

I think this because <u>he has packages in a truck and is checking off a list</u>.

Write *(What is something your family buys that you need?)*

Answers will vary. Possible answers: food, clothes, medicine

Write *(What are three jobs people can do to earn an income?)*

Answers will vary. Possible answers: doctors, tree trimmers, factory workers, bakers, chefs, teachers, lawyers

Practice

Answers will vary. Possible answers:

I would need to buy <u>food, house, and clothes.</u>

I would want to buy <u>games, books, and videos.</u>

Show What You Know

1. B, C, D
2. B, C
3. A, B, C
4. job
5. Income
6. want, need

LESSON 27
Budgets and Saving

Lesson Objectives
By the end of this lesson, your student will be able to:
- define the terms *budget* and *savings*
- describe how income and savings are part of a budget
- evaluate how a budget helps people meet their wants and needs
- describe why people use banks

Supporting Your Student

Explore
Help your student think of a meal and discuss the meal with your student. Help your student find those ingredients online. You can also help with the calculations, if needed.

Read *(Budgeting Wants and Needs)*
Explain how people need food, shelter, and water first before their wants like vacations and toys. Explain to your student how shelter could be an apartment or a house. People pay money each month to buy a house or pay rent. Remember that food can be both a need and a want. Desserts are wants because we do not need to eat those to survive. However, vegetables are needed because they have the vitamins and minerals that our bodies need.

Take a Closer Look
You may need to explain each situation to your student in more detail, especially concerning a bank account. People must open an account, and it has the person's name on it. Then the people at the bank keep track of how much money they put into that account and how much they take out.

Write *(Think of some jobs that people do to make an income. What do they do to get the income?)*
Describe some jobs that your student may or may not know, like doctor, mechanic, dentist, and barber, and what they do. Then, explain to your student that these people make money in the form of a paycheck. They get that paycheck every week, two weeks, or longer.

Learning Styles

Auditory learners may enjoy listening to people describe their budgets. This will allow your student to become more aware of the types of bills that adults pay for each month. Your student may also enjoy listening to a podcast that explains budgets and using a budget to pay for different wants and needs. They might also enjoy explaining how to open a bank account and begin saving money and explaining what special purpose or item the money is being saved for, if any.

Visual learners may enjoy creating a budget using a chart to show the income and bills.

Kinesthetic learners may enjoy pretending to help pay for supplies for an event that is coming up by using a budget.

Extension Activities

Should We Buy This?
Find a few items in your house such as packaged food, books, a cell phone, bottled water, and a toy. Label each item a certain amount of money, but do not exceed $10. Give your student $20 in pretend money or money that you have created out of paper. Tell your student that they only have $20 to "spend" on these items. First, ask your student what types of items should be bought first (needs or wants). Then ask your student to select an item to "buy" with the $20. Your student may buy as many things as they have money for. Remind your student that they could also save some of the money rather than spending it all.

At the Bank
Take your student to the bank and show them how to open an account, and how to keep track of putting money in an account. Another suggestion would be to look at a sample of an account where money is deposited and withdrawn. Explain to your student how money is deposited and withdrawn. The amount of money in the account will increase when money is deposited and decrease when money is withdrawn. Also, explain to your student about earning interest at the bank. Saving money is useful because people who have these savings accounts earn interest.

LESSON 27
Budgets and Saving

Answer Key

Explore
Answers may vary. Possible answer: Hamburger buns $1.50, hamburger patties $5.00, mustard $2.50, ketchup $2.50, cheese $3.00

Write *(Think of some jobs that people do to make an income. What do they do to get the income?)*
Answers may vary. Possible answer: Some jobs that people do to make an income are teacher, doctor, and barber. Teachers go to school and teach their students for an income. Doctors treat patients, and barbers cut hair to get an income.

Take a Closer Look
1. savings
2. interest
3. budget
4. account
5. income
6. bank

Practice
Answers will vary.

Show What You Know
7. True
8. False
9. True
10. True
11. False
12. True
13. False
14. True

LESSON 28
Taxes

Lesson Objectives
By the end of this lesson, your student will be able to:
- describe how taxes are collected from people and businesses
- explain how communities and governments use tax money

Supporting Your Student

Explore
Help your student identify the items in the picture. The raspberries cost $5.00 per box, and the figs cost $6.00 per box. Also, discuss with your student about your last trip to a store. Discuss how you paid tax or a little extra. If possible, show a receipt with the tax on it.

Write *(Explain the three different types of taxes. Describe the situation in which someone would have to pay an income tax, a sales tax, and a property tax.)*
If your student is struggling with explaining a situation, after they identify the three different types of taxes, ask, "Where is the income tax taken out? Where are you when you pay sales tax? What is property?"

Read *(Who Gets Tax Money?)*
Discuss with your student the differences between the community, the state government, and the federal government. The community takes care of local issues like the streets and buildings in the community. The state government takes care of roads and buildings that are owned by the state. The federal government takes care of the nation and things that apply to the whole nation like the military and health care.

Practice
Reassure your student that there are some uses that are the same for both the community and the government. Ask your student to review which ones would be the same.

Learning Styles

Auditory learners may enjoy listening to or watching a video about taxes. There are many videos online for kids that explain taxes. Your student may also enjoy creating their own podcast about taxes.

Visual learners may enjoy creating their own paycheck by drawing a paycheck and including the income tax reduced from the amount. Your student may also enjoy creating an infographic about taxes.

Kinesthetic learners may enjoy buying items at a store and figuring out what sales tax is applied to the total amount of the items.

Extension Activities

Your Kingdom's Tax Law
Have your student pretend they are in charge of a kingdom. They must tax their citizens. Have your student create their kingdom's own tax law. Have them consider who they will tax. How much will they tax them? Will they make them pay an income tax, sales tax, or property tax?

Tax Pictures
Find pictures of receipts, people buying items in a store, or purchasing boats, cars, or homes. Also, find images of people receiving their paychecks at work, or show them a real paycheck. Then have your student identify the type of tax in each picture (income, sales, or property).

Answer Key

LESSON 28
Taxes

Explore
You will spend more than $11.00 even though the two amounts together equal $11.00. You will pay an extra amount because you have to pay a tax.

Write *(Explain three different types of taxes. Describe the situation in which someone would have to pay an income tax, a sales tax, and a property tax.)*
Answers may vary. Possible answers: Income tax is money taken out of a paycheck. People at work would see this tax. A sales tax is added to an item that you buy at a store. A property tax is extra money you have to pay for expensive items like houses, cars, and boats. You pay this tax each year.

Practice
Types of Taxes: income, sales, property

Taxes Used by the Community: police/law enforcement, roads, buildings, education, environment, health care

Taxes Used by the Government: health care, helping people after disasters, military

Show What You Know
1. Income
2. sales
3. property
4. paycheck
5. Taxes
6. A
7. C

LESSON 29
Chapter 3 Review

Lesson Objectives

By the end of this lesson, your student will review the following big ideas from Chapter 3.

- The three types of resources are natural, human, and capital. Natural resources are found in nature. Human resources are the people who work to make the goods and provide the services. Capital resources are goods produced and used to make other goods. (Lesson 23)
- Goods are items that are produced and can be touched. Services are acts that people do for others to help or make money. (Lesson 24)
- Goods and services can be either wants or needs. (Lesson 25)
- Currency is a system of money like dollars and cents. Besides using currency, people can also barter to get goods and services. (Lesson 26)
- A budget is a list of a person's needs and wants and how much they will spend on them each month. (Lesson 27)
- The three types of taxes include sales, income, and property. Taxes are paid to the community or government. (Lesson 28)

Supporting Your Student

Write *(Name a good that you consume. Explain why you consume it.)*
After your student chooses a good, describe what *consume* means. It means something that must be replaced after using it one time or it is used over and over again. Toys are goods that are used over and over again. We do not play with them once and then throw them away. Discuss with your student whether the good they picked is gone after one use or if they use it over and over again.

Review *(Barter and Currency)*
You may want to role-play bartering. Collect an item of yours that you think your student might enjoy. Have your student do the same. Then, see if the two of you want to exchange those items. If you both agree, then explain how this is bartering.

Practice *(Barter and Currency Venn Diagram)*
Discuss with your student the steps to bartering and what it includes. Write those down so both you and your student can see the list. Then list what is included in using currency to get goods. Discuss what differences you see in those lists and the similarities that you see in those lists.

Learning Styles

Auditory learners may enjoy listening to someone in your family describe how they created their family's budget. The family member may explain what wants and needs are included each month to pay the bills and the things that they want to buy. Also, the family member may describe how much goes into savings.

Visual learners may enjoy looking at different receipts and paychecks to find where taxes are added or taken out.

Kinesthetic learners may enjoy drawing or creating a comic strip online about the system of getting money through an income and paying for goods and services.

Extension Activities

Tax Skit
Create a skit or have your student create a skit about making an income and paying taxes in certain situations (at a store for sales tax, receiving a paycheck for income tax, living in a home and paying a property tax). One person will be paying the taxes, and the other person will be the government collecting and using the taxes.

Analyzing Currency
With your student, look online for different types of currency. Have them research and find what other countries' currencies look like today. They could also see what currency looked like hundreds of years ago.

Answer Key

LESSON 29
Chapter 3 Review

Write *(Name a good that you consume. Explain why you consume it.)*
Answers will vary. Possible answer: Paper is a good that you consume. I consume it because once I use it, then I will throw it away. Paper is a want.

Write *(A friend has a toy that you would like. Explain how you would barter with that friend.)*
Answers will vary. Possible answer: I would ask the friend if they would like to trade their toy for my blanket. If the friend agrees, then we will make the trade.

Write *(How are taxes collected from people? How are they used?)*
Answers will vary. Possible answer: Taxes are collected in three ways. People who have jobs receive an income and are taxed with an income tax. People who buy items pay a sales tax, and people who own houses, boats, and cars pay a property tax each year. The community and government gets the tax money to repair streets, pay for the military, and pay for health care.

Practice *(Resources Graphic Organizer)*
Teal box: economy

Blue box 1: natural resources

Blue box 2: human resources

Blue box 3: capital resources

Blue box 4: goods

Blue box 5: services

Practice *(Barter and Currency Venn Diagram)*
Answers will vary. Possible answers:

Barter: only uses goods or services, no money, does not take place in a store

Currency: uses money, usually takes place in a store

Both: receives goods or services, must provide something in return

CHAPTER 3
Assessment

Quick Review

Refer to the statement your student circled in the Show What You Know section to self-assess their knowledge of the chapter concepts. Then to assist in determining if your student is ready to take the assessment, consider:

- Having your student describe the differences among the types of resources.
- Having your student explain that a budget includes what you pay for and your income.
- Having your student explain that taxes are used for roads, buildings, and health care for both the community and the government.

CHAPTER 3
Assessment

Chapter Assessment

Project: Picture

In this project, your student will show a group of scenes through pictures to recreate and show the three types of resources, goods and services, needs and wants, bartering and using currency, budgeting, and taxes. Your student will create a scene with other people, props, and whatever is needed to create the scene for each situation below. Then have them take a picture of it using a camera or a cell phone. The pictures can be digital or printed out. Then the student will write a sentence about what is happening in each scene.

Project Requirements or Steps:

1. Create a picture for each of these situations:

    a. Show the three types of resources

    b. Show an example of a good being bought or a service being provided

    c. Show one need and one want that would be on a budget

    d. Show two people bartering

    e. Show one way how tax money is collected and used

2. Think about what each situation means and should include.
3. Draw a picture of how each scene should be created.
4. Create the background for each situation.
5. Identify props needed for each scene.
6. Find extra people, if needed, for each scene.
7. Create each scene.
8. Take a picture of the scene with a camera or cell phone.
9. Paste the picture either on paper or digitally.
10. Write a sentence for each scene about what is happening in the scene.

CHAPTER 3
Assessment

Chapter Assessment Rubric

Use the following rubric to grade your student's assessment.

	4	3	2	1	Points
Pictures	The scene is created and easily understood by the viewer. The scene shows exactly what should be happening in each scene using people and props.	The scene is created and somewhat easy to understand. The scene shows most of what should be happening in each scene using people and props.	The scene is created, but the student will most likely have to explain what is happening in each scene.	The scene may not be created fully, and it may not be known or understood what is happening in each scene.	
Sentence Descriptions	A complete sentence with clear details was written fully explaining the situation in each scene.	A sentence with some details was written explaining the situation in each scene.	A sentence with a few details was written explaining some of the situation in each scene.	A sentence with limited details was written explaining a few or no parts of the situation in each scene.	
Grammar and Mechanics	There are no grammar or punctuation errors.	There are one or two grammar or punctuation errors.	There are several grammar or punctuation errors.	There are a distracting number of grammar or punctuation errors.	

Total Points _____/12

Average _____

CHAPTER 3
Assessment

Alternative Assessment

Circle the correct answer for each question.

1. How do natural, human, and capital resources impact people in a community?

   A. They provide money to the people.
   B. They help people live, work, and play.
   C. They help people get goods and services.
   D. They help people learn better.

2. Which of the following is a need?

   A. cake
   B. vegetables
   C. toy
   D. television

3. Which of the following is a want?

   A. air
   B. shelter
   C. cell phone
   D. food

4. If someone does not have money, how can they still get goods and services?

   A. barter
   B. use currency
   C. consume
   D. provide services

5. What do people get for going to work and doing their job?

   A. an economy
   B. trading
   C. wants
   D. income

6. How does a budget help people meet their wants and needs?

   A. It makes sure people pay their wants first.
   B. It makes sure people put money into a savings account.
   C. It makes sure people pay their needs first.
   D. It allows people to make more money.

7. How are the three types of taxes collected from people?

   A. by a paycheck, government, and community
   B. from natural disasters, military, and damages
   C. through their houses, boats, and cars
   D. through income, sales, and property

8. True or False Examples of a service are shirts and pants.

9. True or False An example of a good is cutting someone's grass for money in return.

10. True or False Goods can be needs or wants.

11. True or False People need the service of the police officer.

CHAPTER 3
Assessment

12. True or False — When someone works a job, they give income to the company.

13. True or False — Savings is the money left over after spending.

14. True or False — A budget uses a person's income to know how much to use for their wants, needs, and savings.

15. True or False — Tax money is used to pay for health care, roads, buildings, environment, and law enforcement.

16. True or False — The community uses tax money for the military and natural disasters.

Fill in the blanks using the words from the Word Bank.

Word Bank natural   capital   human   goods   services   economy   budget   bank   government

17. _____ resources let people live because they include air and water.

18. _____ resources are tools and machines that let people make things.

19. _____ resources are people who work to make the goods and provide the services that people need to survive.

20. _____ are items that are produced and can be touched.

21. _____ are acts that people do for others to help or make money.

22. _____ is a system of money like dollars and cents.

23. People create a _____ since it is a list of a person's needs and wants and how much they will spend on them each month.

24. People create an account at a _____ to save their extra money for later.

25. The _____ receives tax money to pay for the military.

CHAPTER 3
Assessment

Alternative Assessment Answer Key

1. B
2. B
3. C
4. A
5. D
6. C
7. D
8. False
9. False
10. True
11. True
12. False
13. True
14. True
15. True
16. False
17. Natural
18. Capital
19. Human
20. Goods
21. Services
22. Economy
23. budget
24. bank
25. government

LESSON 30
The Land Around Us

Lesson Objectives

By the end of this lesson, your student will be able to:
- identify and describe features of your local environment
- compare and contrast an aerial photograph of an area with a map
- compare and contrast environmental features of different locations

Supporting Your Student

Read *(Mapping the World Around Us)*
Support interaction with lesson material by having your student observe as many types of maps as possible. Discuss the different types of information provided in each map observed. Some maps show borders, or the political divisions of the land. Others show geographical features or the physical makeup of the land. Some maps have both or neither! If your student struggles to name which type of information is being displayed in a given map, prompt them to look at the details in the map and think about what these details are showing. For example, the color blue on a map shows water, while brown, tan, and green show land. A gray line might show a road on a city map.

Read *(Views of Our World)*
Help your student locate the similarities and differences between the photograph and map of London by focusing on a particular feature to see how it is displayed in each one. For example, the river in the photograph is shown winding across the land. Have your student trace the river with their finger and describe its color. Point out that the river looks real. Compare it to a river your student may have seen. Next, find the river on the map. Have your student trace the river with their finger and describe its color. Point out that the path of the river may be slightly different. This is because the map is a drawing and not the real river. Also, discuss how the river is blue on the map when it does not look blue on the photograph. This is because maps can use general colors to describe land and water. Water, no matter what it looks like in real life, is usually shown as blue on a map.

Practice

Help your student look at the different features of each environment shown. Guide your student with leading questions about each photograph individually, such as "What does the land look like?," "Is there any water?," "What does the water look like?," or "Do you see any plants or animals?" Have your student think about how their descriptions were the same and different. Prompt them to develop these ideas by asking questions such as "What was the same about the land?" or "What was different?"

Learning Styles

Auditory learners may enjoy listening to or creating geography, map, or neighborhood songs related to lesson content. These songs could describe the environmental features of the area. Challenge your student to create a song about the environmental features of where they live.

Visual learners may enjoy working with an online interactive map that allows them to toggle between views. This will provide them a way of observing the same place through multiple lenses: political map, physical map, road map, topographical map, etc. Visual learners may also appreciate similar interactions with available satellite imagery of their community.

Kinesthetic learners may enjoy the chance to get outside to explore their neighborhood firsthand. They could consider counting how many steps it takes to walk around the block or timing how long it takes to travel to the nearest park.

Extension Activities

Map Bingo
With your student, think of 24 features of a community to fill a 5x5 Bingo board (the middle square is a free space). Features should be general, such as a park playground, capitol building, cul-de-sac, bridge, bike path, hiking trail, etc. Keep the bingo cards in the car and pull them out to play when visiting a new place. Your student can mark off the

LESSON 30
The Land Around Us

features they see until they get five in a row!

Map Navigation

Involve your student in any use of GPS technology. Have your student aid in the reading of GPS navigation tools whenever they are used, such as during long car trips.

Answer Key

Explore

Answers may vary depending on where your student lives.

Write *(Make a list of the natural and human-made things that you see.)*

Answers may vary. Possible answers:

Natural	Human-Made
Grass / Land	Roads
Trees	Buildings
Pond / Lake	Vehicles

Practice

Answers will vary. Possible answers:

Desert: has dry land, no plants, no water, looks brown

Both: land seems to be mostly flat, show land

Forest: has trees, very green, has a river, has a lot of water

Show What You Know

1. B
2. A
3. C
4. B, C
5. A
6. Answers will vary depending on your student's environment. Possible answers: roads, ponds, lakes, streams, rivers, mountains, hills, valleys, buildings.

LESSON 31
The Environments of Our World

Lesson Objectives

By the end of this lesson, your student will be able to:

- describe how the environment changes the way people live in an area

Supporting Your Student

Explore
Before starting this section, it will be helpful to read through the vocabulary words and review the four seasons with your student. Ask them how we dress differently and do different activities during each season. This will help build their background knowledge and connect to the lesson material.

Read *(Environmental Factors)*
It will be helpful to bookmark the environmental factors list. As you read through the following sections, ask your student which environmental factor influenced the way the people lived. For example, when reading about the Sahara Desert in the section "How the Environment Changes the Way People Live," it says that "people wear loose-fitting, long-sleeved shirts and pants to keep them protected from the sand and sun while also keeping them cool," so you can have your student connect their clothing to the factors of temperature and the region's characteristics (the sand). Doing so can help your student understand some of the specific ways that an environment can change the way that people live and why people must make these changes in order to live in that environment successfully.

Write *(Why might people have to change the way that they live when moving to a new area?)*
It may be helpful to have your student create a list of things that might have to change if they moved to a new area. Then afterward, have your student select one or two items to write into a sentence and tell why those changes would need to be made.

Learning Styles

Auditory learners may enjoy sections being read aloud, interviewing people who live in different places about how the environment affects them, or creating a podcast about the different types of environments and the ways that the people who live in them must adapt to those environments.

Visual learners may enjoy photos of different environments, video lessons on different environmental factors, or drawing different people in different environments.

Kinesthetic learners may enjoy highlighting the vocabulary words, using sticky notes to write notes on, and having real-life objects needed in different environments, like sun hats for summer and gloves for winter.

Extension Activities

Compare and Contrast
Draw a Venn diagram for your student to compare two different environments. It could be a hot versus cold environment, desert versus tropical environment, or Plains (Midwest United States) versus Coastal towns. What are the similarities? What are the differences?

Draw Different Habitats
Have your student choose two habitats to draw. After your student finishes their drawings, discuss how they are different and what environmental factors would influence the way people live there.

Habitats: desert, arctic, tropical rainforest, temperate forest, grasslands

LESSON 31
The Environments of Our World

Answer Key

Explore
Answers will vary. Possible answers are included in the chart below.

Environmental Factor	Human's Action
Lives by the ocean	Eats fish
Very hot weather	Goes swimming to cool down, wears sun protection
Lives in the forest with many trees	Uses lumber to build homes, learns to climb trees
Snowy landscape	Wears winter clothing, uses sleds, builds fires

Write (*How do environmental factors affect the lives of the people in your community?*)
Answers will vary. Possible answers: I live where the temperature changes, so I have different clothes for the seasons. I live in an area with a lot of people, so there are a lot of apartment buildings. I live where it is really warm all year long, so we have air-conditioning in our homes.

Write (*Why might people have to change the way that they live when moving to a new area?*)
Answers will vary. Possible answers: If moving to a colder climate, our homes would need to be built to keep us warm, and the clothes would change to better live in the new environment.

Practice
Color the items you would use if you lived in the hot desert (answer marked with the crayon).

Circle the items you would use if you lived in the cold tundra of Alaska (answer marked with a circle).

Show What You Know
1. C
2. A
3. A
4. C
5. D
6. B
7. Answers will vary. Possible answers:

   A. Temperature: People have to wear different types of clothes if it is cold or hot.

   B. Location to resources: If water or food are far away, people need to learn how to store food and water.

   C. Population density: The number of people will affect how much of the resources they will use and need.

   D. Landscape: The landscape affects how people travel and build their homes.

   E. Habitat: Different habitats are the tundra (low temperatures and short growing seasons), desert (driest places on Earth), forest (many trees and animals), and tropical (warm temperatures and lots of rain): Depending on the habitat, it affects what types of resources they have and what people eat.

LESSON 32
Adapting to Our Environment

Lesson Objectives

By the end of this lesson, your student will be able to:

- identify ways people adapt to the environment where they live

Supporting Your Student

Explore
It may be helpful to create a list of things that people might do based on the weather outside. For example, when it is snowing, we wear warm clothes, shovel the walkway, and put chains on the car. This will help your student to answer the explore question and build prior knowledge about adaptations that could help your student connect to and understand the lesson more easily and effectively.

Read *(Three Ways Humans Adapt)*
Bookmark this page to refer to throughout the lesson. When reading about adaptations, you can refer to the chart to see what type of adaptation it is. Then ask your student guided questions to help them understand the characteristics of each type of adaptation better. For example, "Plumbing is a way we direct water from a fresh water source to our homes. What kind of adaptation is this?" It would be environmental because humans changed the flow of water.

Write *(What is one change to your behavior your environment has influenced recently?)*
Use the table "Examples of Behavior Adaptations" to help generate ideas to answer the question. Encourage your student to come up with new ideas.

Practice
Use the Read "Three Ways Humans Adapt" section as a reference when sorting the changes.

Learning Styles

Auditory learners may enjoy sections being read aloud to them or enjoy discussing different adaptations with the instructor. They may also enjoy listening to or creating a podcast about the different types of adaptations.

Visual learners may enjoy the tables and graphic organizers within the lesson and may enjoy looking at photos of different communities to see how they adapted the land. They might also enjoy creating drawings or posters that show people adapting to their environments in different ways.

Kinesthetic learners may enjoy going on a walk and finding different adaptations to the environment or environmental factors that influence their behavior.

Extension Activities

Interview a Family Member
Have your student interview a family member who lives or has lived in a different location. Have them ask the following questions:

- What is the weather like there? What type of clothing do you need?
- What are the unique characteristics of this place?
- What is something special people do to live there?
- What type of animals live there?
- What are the buildings mostly made from?
- What is a popular food?

Create a Comic Strip
Have your student create a comic strip of a person moving to a new habitat. The beginning should depict the environmental factors of the area, the middle should depict behavioral changes that the person makes, and the end should depict environmental changes that the person makes.

LESSON 32
Adapting to Our Environment

Answer Key

Explore
Answers will vary. Possible answers: putting on certain clothes based on the weather, packing food if I'm going to be away for a long time, changing plans because of the rain

Write *(What is one biological adaptation humans have made?)*
Answers will vary. Possible answers: walking on two legs, endurance running, sweating

Write *(What is one change to your behavior your environment has influenced recently?)*
Answers will vary. Possible answers: putting sunscreen on, wearing a hat, turning on a fan

Practice

Biological	Behavioral	Environmental
Sweating	Putting a coat on	Building a house
Building muscles	Wearing a hat	Farming

Show What you Know
1. B
2. C
3. A
4. True
5. Adaptations

LESSON 33
Jobs Around the World

Lesson Objectives

By the end of this lesson, your student will be able to:

- explain how the jobs where you live may depend on the environment
- identify a job specific to a certain environment

Supporting Your Student

Create

To help your student be successful, begin by planning out the diorama. Encourage your student to select an environment first. Talk about different environments that might be fun to model. A forested community, a coastal town, a desert, or a mountainous environment are all ideas your student could select. Discussing landforms and different environments with which your student is familiar will give your student an idea of what they would like to make. You can also discuss the three types of communities (rural, urban, suburban) studied previously. Your student's diorama can focus on one of these types of communities as well. Once a specific environment has been selected, make a list of different jobs people do in the chosen environment. Then have your student select one.

Help your student get started on the building of the project by collecting materials together. As you organize materials, discuss how each will be used in the completion of the project.

Remember, projects that are completed over time can be frustrating for some students. Discuss the idea of a long-term project with your student. Explain that you may only complete a small part of the project each day. Write a schedule together or print out and use the one below:

- Day One: Brainstorm ideas for your diorama and collect materials.
- Day Two: Paint or color the background for your diorama.
- Day Three: Design the three-dimensional figures you will place in your diorama.

Explore

In this exploration, your student is asked to think about jobs done in their environment that cannot be done somewhere else. Your student may need prompting and assistance here. Make a list of jobs in the community and discuss or draw a map of the community together to help your student recall or visualize the resources and landforms present. Point out that because there are unique or specific resources, landforms, and human-made features, there are certain jobs that are specific to their environment.

Take a Closer Look

In selecting a person to interview, your student may need guidance to make the activity relevant. Talk about family members and friends who might have a job that depends on the environment. Following the interview, discuss the subject's answers and whether their job depends on the environment. Ask why the job depends on the environment or why not.

Learning Styles

Auditory learners may enjoy an ears-only activity. Ask your student to close their eyes. Describe an environment in detail. Include the resources you see in the environment, but do not name the environment. When you have completed your description, ask your student to open their eyes and name the specific environment. Switch roles.

Visual learners may enjoy making flash cards with drawings of environments on one side and jobs that depend on the environments on the other.

Kinesthetic learners may enjoy a point and talk exercise. Put your hands behind your back and tell your student that they are in charge of pointing. Use a photograph found in the worktext or online to talk about the features and natural resources you see in an environment. Ask your student to point to features in the photograph as you describe them. They may also enjoy playing a game of statue. Name an environment, and tell your student to jump, skip, or dance until they hear the name of a job that depends on that environment. When they hear the name of the job, they must freeze like a statue!

LESSON 33
Jobs Around the World

Extension Activities

Mural Making
Make a mural with your student illustrating different environments and jobs done in each.

Dramatization
Pretend that you have a job opening in a certain environment. Explain the duties of your employees and how they work with the natural resources in the environment. Have your student interview for the job! Switch roles.

Answer Key

Explore
Answers will vary. Your student should describe landforms such as streams, rivers, mountains, and forests as well as human-made features such as city streets, bridges, freeways, and schools. Your student should identify jobs such as cashiers in stores, librarians, and teachers.

In the Real World
This job cannot be done in every community. Other fishermen can work in coastal, ocean areas. Answers will vary. Encourage your student to name specific ocean or lake environments they may have experience visiting.

Write *(What type of job would you like to have? Describe the environment you need to do this work.)*
Answers will vary, but your student should describe the type of job that they would like to have and the environment that would be necessary to do this job.

Write *(Each of these specific environments has natural resources that help workers do their jobs. Describe another specific environment and its natural resources. What job depends on the environment that you described?)*
Answers will vary. Possible answers: A Sherpa takes mountain climbers into the Himalayas. This job depends on the beautiful yet rugged and dangerous mountains. A wildlife photographer depends on natural environments such as the forests and mountains of Yosemite.

Practice
Fisherman: Harbor/coastal environment

Taxi Driver: Urban community/city environment

Farmer: Rural community/flat land environment

Lumberjack: Forest environment

Write *(Marine biologists are scientists who study animals living in the sea. What environment do you think these workers do their job in?)*
Marine biologists do their jobs in environments that have water.

Show What you Know
1. False
2. D
3. Answers may vary. Possible answer: If you are a farmer, you need an environment with plenty of open space, flat land, and healthy soil for growing crops.
4. Answers will vary. Marine biologists, fishermen, sailors, and lifeguards all depend on an ocean environment.

LESSON 34
Different Jobs in Different Places

Lesson Objectives
By the end of this lesson, your student will be able to:
- define the word *climate*
- describe the climate of your area
- explain how the jobs in an area may depend on the area's climate and geography

Supporting Your Student

Create
If your student does not remember what the typical weather is like during each season, you can help by looking up images online. Brainstorm what the sky looks like during the winter, spring, summer, and fall. What do leaves look like? Encourage your student to include all of these details in their artwork. If your student would prefer to draw a picture of a building other than their home, they can do that too! A church, a store, or even a tree can be used as the centerpiece.

Encourage your student to use the Create artwork they complete to answer questions regarding their own climate if they struggle to answer the questions in this lesson.

Read *(Climate: Weather Over Time)*
Your student may need further explanation to fully understand the difference between climate and weather. Pause often during the reading to ask questions and provide explanation. Asking questions like "What is the weather like today?" and "What is the weather usually like this time of year?" can help provide clarity. Explain that we use much of the same vocabulary to discuss weather and climate. Words like *rainy*, *warm*, and *cold* can describe both weather and climate. Time words like *yesterday*, *today*, and *tomorrow* are hints that weather is being discussed. Time words like *usually*, *most of the time*, *often*, *this time of year*, and *during the winter* are words and phrases that tell us climate is being discussed.

Read *(Jobs Depend on Climate and Geography)*
Your student may have limited knowledge of pinwheels and wind turbines. You can draw a picture of a pinwheel or look up an example online to show your student that these decorations have sails that move due to the wind. (See Pinwheel extension activity below for a fun way to continue this learning experience.)

Learning Styles

Auditory learners may enjoy making weather sounds and having you mimic the weather when you read weather and climate words. What does a windy climate sound like? What does a rainy climate sound like?

Visual learners may enjoy making drawings of different climates and using these visuals to answer climate questions and to match up with photographs in the worktext.

Kinesthetic learners may enjoy researching weather words in sign language, and then using these signs to respond to climate and weather questions. Your student can also have fun creating a dance or hand sign to represent each type of climate.

Extension Activities

Pinwheel
Make pinwheels to draw conclusions about the wind and to confirm whether your student lives in a windy climate. You will need a square piece of paper, scissors, glue or tape, a straw or pencil with an eraser on the end, and a brad fastener or paperclip. Build the pinwheel according to the directions below. Then monitor or observe your student's pinwheel. Ask your student to keep a wind log and record the pinwheel's movements every day for one week, four times throughout the day. If the wind causes the pinwheel to spin a great deal and with speed each day, your student may live in a windy climate. If your pinwheel rarely moves, your student does not live in a windy climate.

Here are the steps for building your pinwheel:

1. Holding one of the square paper's corners, fold it to meet the opposite corner. Open the folded paper and repeat with the other two corners. Your folds should make four visible triangles on the square paper. The folds should intersect in the center of the paper.

LESSON 34
Different Jobs in Different Places

2. Cut along each of the four the folds from the outer edge toward the center of the paper where the folds intersect. Cut two-thirds of the way toward the center of the square. Then stop.

3. Take a pencil and make a dot in the center of your paper. Glue one corner of a triangle to the center of the square, gluing the very tip of the corner you pulled to the center. When the tip is fully glued and does not pull away from the center, repeat this step with the same corner of the next triangle. Repeat the process with all four triangles.

4. Your paper should now look like a pinwheel, but it still needs a cylinder of some kind to hold it upright. Push a brad fastener, paperclip, or pin through the center of the paper and into the top of a straw or the eraser on a pencil.

5. Find a place outside to push the straw or pencil into the ground, so the pinwheel stands upright and can spin in the wind. Blow the sails of your pinwheel to make sure it will spin in the wind.

Bar Graph
Help your student create a bar graph showing their friends' and family members' favorite types of weather. Your student should ask each person whether they prefer hot, mild, cold, rainy, windy, or snowy weather. Your student can call friends and family on the phone to find out their favorite types of weather. They can ask friends who come over to play too! Encourage your student to collect as many responses as possible to make your bar graph interesting.

LESSON 34

Different Jobs in Different Places

Ask your student follow-up questions, such as, "Which type of weather do most people prefer? Why do people prefer that type of weather? Which type of weather do you prefer?"

Use your student's bar graph as a link to mathematics concepts!

Answer Key

Explore
Answers will vary. Encourage your student to use appropriate weather words to describe the climate in their answer.

Write *(How are climates different around the world? Do all climates experience changes in the weather each season?)*
Answers will vary. Possible answers: Tropical and polar climates do not change very much from season to season. Quebec has a temperate climate with changing seasons while the climate in the Amazon Rainforest does not change. It stays hot and humid all year long.

Show What You Know
1. B
2. C
3. True
4. Answers may vary. Possible answers: Lifeguards depend on the ocean and a warm climate. The climate at the beach is warm and sunny most of the year, and many people like to swim in warm climates. Ski instructors depend on mountains and cold, snowy climates. The mountain climate is where people like to learn how to ski because of its snow.

LESSON 35
Climate Changes Our Communities

Lesson Objectives

By the end of this lesson, your student will be able to:

- describe how the climate of an area can change the way people live, work, or play in a community

Supporting Your Student

Read *(Types of Climates)*
As your student reads this section, it may be helpful to search for images or videos of tropical and polar environments by using an online search engine. For example, tropical climates are usually wet, hot, humid, or dry. Have your student observe these features by showing them photos or videos of tropical rainforests. Encourage your student to relate tropical climates to any experiences they may have had in real life. For example, if your student has ever felt rain on a hot and humid day, then they've already experienced a feature of tropical climates.

Write *(Circle the regions on the map that have tropical and polar climates. Name a continent that has a tropical climate.)*
Check your student's understanding of the climate map by making sure they circle regions in the world that are shaded orange (tropical) and blue (polar). Then encourage your student to answer the second question by focusing only on the orange colors on the climate map. If your student is not familiar with the names of the continents in the world, use an online search engine to look for a world map. Encourage your student to identify one continent that features tropical climates, such as parts of North America, South America, Africa, Asia, and Australia.

Practice
Encourage your student to fill in the table by focusing on one column at a time. First, have your student draw a feature of tropical or polar climates. For example, your student may draw palm trees for tropical climates and polar bears for polar climates. Then have your student review the worktext and identify the features of tropical and polar climates. Features of tropical climates include hot and humid, no winter, found in areas along the equator, and wet or dry. Last, have your student identify how climates affect people's work, job, and play. For example, it is difficult for vegetation to grow in polar climates. Therefore, people have jobs as seal hunters and ice fishers to provide food for the community.

Learning Styles

Auditory learners may enjoy listening to a podcast on the different types of climates in the world.

Visual learners may enjoy watching a documentary on global climate change and how it can affect people and the environment.

Kinesthetic learners may enjoy creating a map of the world using modeling clay and designate tropical and polar climates by using two distinct colors.

Extension Activities

The Tale of Two Thermometers
To learn more about global climate change, help your student to set up two thermometers. Then have your student follow these steps:

1. Lay both thermometers in a sunny area outside for a few minutes.
2. Mark down the time and the temperatures of both thermometers on a record sheet.
3. Place a glass or vase in the sun with a thermometer in it. Cover it with plastic wrap or a dark t-shirt.
4. Place the second thermometer next to the glass or vase (not in the shade).
5. Ask your student to form a hypothesis about what will happen to the thermometers by using an If/Then statement. For example, "If the thermometer next to the glass is left in the sun for 30 minutes, then its temperature will be higher than the thermometer in the covered glass."
6. Record the temperatures on both thermometers every 5 to 10 minutes. Leave both thermometers directly in the sun for at least 30 minutes.
7. Ask your student to record the final readings on the thermometers. Then discuss the following question: Why are the temperatures inside and outside of the glass or vase different?

LESSON 35
Climate Changes Our Communities

Thermometers placed in covered containers produce higher temperatures. This is because gases from the air, such as carbon dioxide, and heat from the sun are trapped in the covered container. Carbon dioxide is a greenhouse gas that traps heat, which can lead to global climate change.

Which Ice Cubes Melt Faster?
With your student, learn how global climate change affects the speed of melting glaciers. To simulate glaciers, use ice cubes and have your student follow these steps:

8. Ask your student to form a hypothesis about which ice cubes will melt faster using an If/Then statement. For example, "If water is poured in with the ice cubes, then it will melt faster."
9. Set up two identical plastic containers or one divided container.
10. Optional: Add food coloring into the ice cubes to see them better. (Coloring makes no difference to the melting of ice cubes.)
11. Place an equal number of ice cubes into each container. Then add a small amount of water (room temperature) in one of the containers.
12. Record the time it takes for the ice cubes in each container to melt.
13. Discuss with your student the following question: Which ice cubes melted faster and why?

Contact with the water causes the ice to melt more quickly. This is because the molecules in water are more tightly packed than the molecules in the air, allowing more contact with the ice and a greater rate of heat transfer.

Answer Key
Explore

Answers will vary. Possible answers: Rain keeps the soil fertile, allowing farmers to grow more crops. Rain is important in the water cycle and the irrigation of crops by farmers. Rain affects the type of clothing and equipment people need to say dry, such as rain jackets and umbrellas. Rain cools the environment that people live in. Rain cleans the air, helping people to breathe better.

Write *(Circle the regions on the map that have tropical and polar climates. Name a continent that has a tropical climate.)*
Answers will vary. Make sure your student circles the regions on the map that are denoted in orange and blue. Continents that have tropical climates include parts of North America, South America, Africa, Asia, and Australia.

Write *(How does global climate change affect people and the environment?)*
Answers will vary. Possible answers: When ice melts, it can disrupt the habitat of fish. If there is not enough fish, it can be hard for people to provide food to the community.

Practice
Answers will vary. Possible answers:

LESSON 35
Climate Changes Our Communities

Climate Type	What That Climate Looks Like	Facts About That Climate	How That Climate Affects How People Live, Work, and Play
Tropical	Palm trees, sun, tropical fruits, or forest animals	Hot and humid; no winter; lots of rain; dry	People don't need heaters in the winter to stay warm; people search for new plants in rainforests to make medicines; people search for new fruits and animals for food
Polar	Ice, glaciers, polar bears, penguins, or snow	Very cold; permafrost	Melting ice affects people's food supply; vegetation is hard to grow in the ice; people use sleds drawn by sled dogs to travel, carry supplies, and play in the snow

Show What You Know
14. tropical climate
15. polar climate
16. A, B, C
17. A, B

LESSON 36
Conserve and Protect Natural Resources

Lesson Objectives

By the end of this lesson, your student will be able to:
- state the meaning of the word *conserve*
- identify responsible uses of natural resources
- explain ways that people can conserve and protect natural resources

Supporting Your Student

Read *(Types and Uses of Natural Resources)*
To help your student better understand natural resources, it may be helpful to find images of renewable and nonrenewable natural resources. For example, as your student reads about fossil fuels, they may wonder why they're nonrenewable. Discuss with them the process of creating fossil fuels by showing them images. Then explain to your student that the textures of fossil fuels are hard because they take millions of years to form beneath the earth.

Read *(Conservation of Natural Resources)*
Help your student better understand the three Rs by locating household items that can be conserved, such as aluminum cans. Have your student examine the aluminum cans and discuss how they can be reused, reduced, and recycled. Your student can reuse aluminum cans by washing them so that they can be used again. Aluminum cans can also be recycled and made into crafts, such as ornaments, models, and figurines. Note: Your student may notice an overlap between the reducing and reusing of items. For example, you can reduce the amount of plastic bag waste by reusing them again. Remind your student that the distinction between the two is not always clear-cut. However, reducing something usually means to reduce waste, and reusing items usually means to use them more than once.

Practice
Have your student complete the table by focusing on one column at a time. For example, have your student fill in the "Drawing" column first. If your student is struggling with the last column, assist them by reviewing the three Rs: reduce, reuse, and recycle. Since your student only needs to identify and write down one of the three Rs, discuss with them how water, for example, can be reused. Encourage your student to think of water in lakes, water bottles, or from a faucet. For example, your student may reason that water is renewable and can be conserved by turning off the faucet whenever water is not needed.

Learning Styles

Auditory learners may enjoy writing a song about how to conserve natural resources.

Visual learners may enjoy watching a documentary on renewable and nonrenewable natural resources.

Kinesthetic learners may enjoy making models or figurines of renewable and nonrenewable natural resources out of modeling clay or other crafting supplies.

Extension Activities

Recycled Tin Can Crafts
Help your student learn the importance of recycling natural resources by creating fun tin can crafts. Your student can turn tin cans into jewelry boxes, planters, bowling pins, organizers, bird feeders, lanterns, wind chimes, animals, pencil holders, drums, and more! Encourage your student to get creative and decorate their crafts to their liking!

Conservation Commercial
Encourage your student to create a commercial on how to conserve natural resources by implementing the three Rs. To do this, have your student select an item they wish to show on camera, such as a soda can. Then encourage your student to demonstrate or discuss how soda cans can be reduced, reused, and recycled. Your student may wish to include parents or siblings in the commercial for a fun and interactive learning process!

LESSON 36
Conserve and Protect Natural Resources

Answer Key

Explore
Answers will vary. Possible answers: I can turn the water off while brushing my teeth. I can use a whiteboard instead of paper. I can turn lights off when I am not using them.

Write *(Name a renewable and a nonrenewable resource. How do people use them?)*
Answers will vary. Possible answers: Renewable resources are water, sunlight, and air. People use water to drink and clean, sunlight as a light source, and air to breathe. Nonrenewable resources are gases, oil, and stone. People use oil to power cars and houses and stone for roads and buildings.

Write *(What are the three Rs? Describe how each step is used for conservation.)*
Answers will vary. Possible answers: The three Rs are reduce, reuse, and recycle. *Reduce* means to lower the amount of waste that is created. For example, people can carry reusable grocery bags. *Reuse* means to use something again instead of throwing it away, like a plastic fork. *Recycle* means to remake it into something else, like aluminum cans melted down and molded to create new cans.

Practice
Answers will vary. Possible answers:

Type of Natural Resource	Drawing	How to Conserve
Oil	varies	Reduce the amount of oil by using alternative energy, like solar energy.
Trees	varies	Paper comes from trees. Recycle by throwing it in recycling bins.
Soil	varies	Reuse by removing plant roots.
Water	varies	Reduce by controlling the amount of water coming out of the faucet.

Show What You Know

1. Answers will vary. Possible answers: Conservation refers to the act of saving and protecting animals, plants, and natural resources.
2. D
3. B
4. B, C, D
5. Answers will vary. Possible answers: Your student may describe or draw a person buying only a few water bottles from the store at a time to explain reducing. Your student may describe or draw a water bottle being washed and used again as an example of reusing. Your student may describe or draw water bottles getting shipped to treatment plants so people can reshape them and create brand new water bottles, water bottles being used for arts and crafts, or water bottles being used as bowling pins as examples of recycling.

LESSON 37
Natural Parks of the World

Lesson Objectives

By the end of this lesson, your student will be able to:

- describe the purposes of national parks
- locate a national park on a map
- locate a park near you on a map)

Supporting Your Student

Write *(What are some of the reasons to have national parks?)*
If your student struggles with listing the reasons to have national parks, ask them to look closely at the images and reread the captions. Prompt them with questions, like, "Why might a national park stop people from cutting down trees?"

Practice
If your student struggles with this practice, remind them to review the compass rose and think about which direction they would go for each statement.

Learning Styles

Auditory learners may enjoy explaining to an adult the benefits of national parks or listening to the different sounds that exist in a national park.

Visual learners may enjoy drawing a picture of a national park, including the landforms, animals, and plants.

Kinesthetic learners may enjoy going on a hike to a natural preserve area. Direct your student to think about why the area may be preserved.

Extension Activities

Field Trip to a National Park
If possible, plan a visit to a national park near you. Encourage your student to take a notebook during the field trip to draw and take notes about what they learn there about the landscape and the wildlife that is being protected there.

Research Project
Choose a national park to study in more detail. Have your student create a multimedia presentation with the information they find about this national park. The presentation could include photographs, video, maps, text, audio narration done by your student, and music.

LESSON 37
Natural Parks of the World

Answer Key

Write *(Preserving means "keeping something alive." Choose a park from the pictures above and write a sentence about what the park preserves.)*
Answers will vary. Possible answer: Serengeti National Park in Africa preserves animals and their habitats.

Write *(What are some of the reasons to have national parks?)*
Answers will vary. Possible answers: to protect the wildlife that lives there, to protect trees from being cut down, to preserve landforms and bodies of water

Practice
If I entered by the east entrance, I would go *west* to get to the lake.

If I entered by the north entrance, I would go *south* to get to Old Faithful.

I would most likely find a moose near the *South* Entrance to the park.

Show What You Know
1. D
2. B
3. C
4. A
5. C

LESSON 38
Chapter 4 Review

Lesson Objectives

By the end of this lesson, your student will review the following big ideas from Chapter 4.

- Maps help us understand the natural and human features of the environment. (Lesson 30)
- The environment changes the way people live. (Lesson 31)
- People find ways to adapt to the environment they live in. (Lesson 32)
- The environment can change the jobs that are available in an area. (Lesson 33)
- The climate can change the jobs that are available in an area. (Lesson 34)
- The climate can change the way people live, work and play. (Lesson 35)
- It is important to use the natural resources from the environment responsibly. (Lesson 36)
- The purpose of national parks is to protect the environment. (Lesson 37)

Supporting Your Student

Write *(Maps of the Environment)*
When your student asks you how to spell a word, prompt them to check the word banks that are available to them. It might also be helpful for them to have a student dictionary available.

Practice *(Adapting to the Environment)*
Before your student fills in the chart, it might be helpful to give them sticky notes with the with these words written on them: jobs, houses, food, clothes and play. Prompt them to go back to the text they read and find some ideas. Then they can copy their ideas on the chart or place the sticky notes on the chart.

Practice *(Taking Care of the Environment)*
Before your student fills in this chart, it might be helpful for them to discuss their ideas with you. You can ask them, "What are some ideas you remember from the text? What are some other ideas you have?"

Learning Styles

Auditory learners may enjoy listening to a podcast about the environment and conservation for kids.

Visual learners may enjoy drawing pictures to illustrate the ways the environment affects people's lives.

Kinesthetic learners may enjoy playing charades with the family using words and concepts from the chapter like environment, weather, climate, human resource, or natural resources.

Extension Activities

Recycled Art
Have your student create some art using discarded things in your house from the recycling bin.

Take Care of the Environment Campaign
Your student can write a song for other children to promote taking care of the environment. The song can include some of the ideas they thought of in the practice section.

Answer Key

Write *(Maps of the Environment)*

LESSON 38
Chapter 4 Review

Possible answers:

Human Features—houses, factories, bridge, buildings

Naturals Features—trees, rivers, ponds, grass

In the Real World

Human resources: house, hammer, furniture, paper, clothes

Natural resources: tree, apple, sunlight, air, water

Practice: Pairs of Words

1. weather
2. climate
3. neighborhood
4. community
5. conserving
6. preserving
7. Circled: windy, rainy, snowy, foggy.
8. Underlined: polar, subtropical, tropical, temperate.

Practice *(Adapting to the Environment)*

Possible answers:

Jobs—Different jobs for different weather or climate like ski instructor or snow removal

Houses—Homes lifted in areas that flood, homes with fireplaces, homes with fans or air conditioning, homes made with the materials available in the area like adobe homes

Food—Different foods grow in different climates, people use the foods that are available in their area

Clothes—People need different clothes for different weather or climate

Play—People do different fun activities like skiing, building snowmen, swimming, surfing

Practice *(Taking Care of the Environment)*

Possible answers:

Water—shorter showers, turn the water off when you brush your teeth, check for leaks, smaller toilets, create less trash to keep the oceans and rivers clean

Air—walking or riding bikes, avoid burning trash, using public transportation, planting trees

Wildlife—planting trees, using recycled paper, going paperless when possible, having a garden, national parks, nature preserve

CHAPTER 4
Assessment

Quick Review

Refer to the statement your student circled in the Show What You Know section to self-assess their knowledge of the chapter concepts. Then to assist in determining if your student is ready to take the assessment, consider:

- Having your student identify natural and human-made features on a map.
- Having your student describe how the environment changes the way people live, work and play. Have your student give examples.
- Having your student describe how climate changes the way people live, work, and play.
- Having your student give examples of natural resources.
- Having your student explain how to use natural resources responsibly.
- Having your student explain the purpose of national parks.

CHAPTER 4
Assessment

Chapter Assessment

Project: Poster

Project Requirements or Steps:

You will create a poster to show ways to take care of the environment. Use your poster to show a chart or diagram that gives information clearly. Use the following steps to create your poster.

1. Select at least two ways to take care of the environment that you studied in the chapter. Gather information about the ways to take care of the environment.
2. Create a title for your poster related to the topic.
3. Include photos and drawings related to the topic.
4. Include information or data to explain and support the photos and drawings you included.
5. Present the information in a creative way.

CHAPTER 4
Assessment

Chapter Assessment Rubric

Use the following rubric to grade your student's assessment.

	4	3	2	1	Points
Connection to the Chapter	The poster is clearly connected to the chapter.	The poster is connected to the chapter.	The poster is somewhat connected to the chapter.	The poster is not connected to the chapter.	
Creativity	The poster is very creative and aesthetically appealing.	The poster is creative and aesthetically appealing.	The poster is somewhat creative and aesthetically appealing.	The poster is not creative or aesthetically appealing.	
Information	The information or data is very accurate and easy to follow.	The information or data is accurate.	The information or data is somewhat accurate.	The information or data is not accurate.	
Grammar and Mechanics	There are no grammar and punctuation mistakes.	There are one or two grammar and punctuation mistakes.	There are several grammar and punctuation mistakes.	There are a distracting number of grammar and punctuation mistakes.	

Total Points _____/16

Average _____

CHAPTER 4
Assessment

Alternative Assessment

1. Draw a map of your region. Include human and nature features on your map.

CHAPTER 4
Assessment

2. Fill in the blanks using the word bank below

   adapt climate environment human natural weather

   A. The _____ changes the way people live, work and play.
   B. People find ways to _____ to their environment.
   C. Mountains, trees, and rivers are examples of _____ features of the environment.
   D. Bridges, houses and roads are examples of _____ features of the environment
   E. _____ is the temperature and outside conditions in a specific place and time.
   F. _____ is the pattern of weather seen over a long period of time.

3. Give an example of how the environment changes the way people work.

   ....

4. Give an example of how the climate changes the way people live.

   ....

5. Give two examples of natural resources.

   ....

   ....

6. Give an example of using a natural resource responsibly.

   ....

7. What is the purpose of national parks?

   ....

CHAPTER 4
Assessment

Alternative Assessment Answer Key

1. Map should show buildings made by people as well as natural features such as plants, landforms or bodies of water.

2. **A.** environment
   B. adapt
   C. natural
   D. human
   E. weather
   F. climate

3. Possible answers: a job could be done differently because of the environment like people who deliver the mail might have to use a different form of transportation

4. Possible answers: houses that are built differently for warmer or colder climates.

5. Possible answers: water, air, trees, sunlight

6. Possible answers: taking shorter showers, using recycled paper, not running the water while brushing teeth

7. Possible answers: to protect the landscape and the wildlife of a place

LESSON 39
What Is Culture?

Lesson Objectives

By the end of this lesson, your student will be able to:
- state the meaning of the word *culture*
- describe ways people show their culture to others

Supporting Your Student

Read *(Cultural Foods and Clothing)*
As your student reads through this section of the worktext, it may be helpful for them to search for additional images of specific foods and clothing by using an online search engine. For example, if your student was interested to see traditional Italian pizza without cheese, they may search for images of margherita pizza, which only contains olive oil, basil leaves, and tomatoes. Similarly, to help your student better visualize traditional clothing from different cultures, have your student look through images of the *agbada* of Nigeria and the *sari* of South Asia. Then, encourage your student to compare these cultural aspects to their own life. Ask them, "Why is culture important to people? How do cultural aspects like foods and clothing affect you?"

Read *(Cultural Greetings and Languages)*
It may be helpful for your student to research different ways people greet each other around the world by using an online search engine. For example, your student may discover that peers in Middle Eastern countries, such as Yemen, United Arab Emirates, and Qatar greet each other by nose bumps. People in South Asian countries, like Thailand, Nepal, and Cambodia greet each other by bowing. Inform your student that people may not only speak different languages but have different expressions when greeting one another. For example, in the United States, people commonly greet each other by saying *hello* or asking someone *how are you?* In Asian countries, people say *hello* by saying *ni hao*, which actually translates to *you good* in English.

Practice *(Table)*
Help your student complete the table by encouraging them to focus on one column at a time. Start by going over the first column, which includes different cultural aspects, such as food, clothing, and greetings/languages. Then have your student draw these descriptions in the second column. For example, your student may draw an olive oil bottle, tomatoes, and basil leaves to denote the ingredients of traditional Italian pizza. In the third column, have your student think about examples of these cultural aspects from their lives. For example, whether your student is from an American background or another cultural background, encourage them to list the unique foods that they eat, the types of clothes that they wear, and the languages that they may speak.

Learning Styles

Auditory learners may enjoy listening to music from different cultures around the world.

Visual learners may enjoy watching a documentary or show on the different types of clothing that people wear around the world.

Kinesthetic learners may enjoy learning some traditional dances from other cultures, such as the salsa of Cuba, samba of Brazil, Bollywood Dance of India, or hula of Hawaii.

Extension Activities

Languages of the World
With your student, research how to say common words, such as *hello* and *goodbye*, in different languages by using an online search engine. Then have your student create a mini book or cheat sheet for travelers by listing additional words and phrases that they think people would need to know. To inspire creativity, you may ask your student to decorate their cheat sheet or mini book. As your student completes this activity, encourage them to think about the different types of words, phrases, and gestures that people might use in other parts of the world.

Cultural Arts and Crafts
With your student, research how to make arts and crafts from a country or geographic region of interest by using an online search engine. For example, if your student wants to learn more about Asian art, they may be interested in creating tissue paper lanterns

LESSON 39
What Is Culture?

or paper fans. If your student wishes to learn more about Native American art, they may be interested in creating paper plate dream catchers. Other examples may include Russian nesting dolls and Brazilian carnival headdresses. As your student completes this activity, encourage them to think about what makes each art or craft piece important to each culture, specifically how they influence people.

Answer Key

Explore
Answers will vary. Ensure your student writes a list of foods they eat during holidays. Also, evaluate your student's response to why they think culture is important. They may respond that culture is important because it identifies who they are, how they fit into the world, accept differences, appreciate similarities, or help people who are different.

Write *(How do people show their culture through the foods that they eat? The clothing that they wear?)*
Answers will vary. Possible answers: People show their culture through the foods that they eat by adding spices and herbs; Men in Nigeria wear robes with wide sleeves called the *agbada*, Women in India wear decorative garments called the *sari*, and Muslim women in the Middle East wear headpieces called the *hijab*.

Write *(How do people show their culture through greetings and language?)*
Answers will vary. Possible answers: People show their culture through greetings, such as shaking hands, waving, bumping noses, or kissing each other on the cheek. They can also greet each other by speaking in different languages and using different expressions.

Practice *(Table)*

Cultural Aspects	Examples From People Around the World	Drawing (what they look like, sound like, or feel like)	Examples From Your Own Life
Food	spices and herbs—basil leaves (Italy); saffron (India); cinnamon (Africa)	Varies	Varies
Clothing	agabra (Nigeria), sari (India), hijab (Middle East)	Varies	Varies
Greetings/ Languages	shaking hands (United States), bumping noses (Middle East), kissing three times on the cheek (the Netherlands); hello (English), ni hao (Chinese)	Varies	Varies

Show What You Know
1. True
2. False
3. False
4. True
5. True
6. agbada
7. blue
8. chopsticks
9. spices

LESSON 40
How Are Cultures Alike and Different?

Lesson Objectives
By the end of this lesson, your student will be able to:
- identify ways people's cultures can be similar and different
- describe your own culture

Supporting Your Student

In the Real World
Help your student find someone they can interview who has different cultural roots than they have, such as a neighbor or friend. Here are some interview questions that your student can ask the interviewee. Your student may also add or revise the suggested list of questions shown below.

- What language(s) do you speak?
- What kind of music do you listen to?
- What kind of clothes do you wear?
- What foods are traditional to your culture?
- What holidays do you celebrate? Do you have any traditions?
- Why is culture important to you?
- Has your culture changed over time?

To record the interviewee's answers, have your student create a video or audio recording of the communication exchange. Alternatively, your student may write down the answers and create a slideshow presentation.

Read *(Holiday Celebrations)*
As your student reads through this section in the worktext, it may be helpful to pull up a world map by using an online search engine. For example, as your student reads about the New Year's Eve celebrations in Japan, Turkey, and Denmark, have your student locate these countries on the map. Ask your student to estimate the distances between these countries to help them get a sense of the nearby countries that might share similar traditions. Then encourage your student to think about the similarities and differences between these three unique cultures and how they compare to their own culture.

Write *(How are wedding celebrations similar and different around the world? How are weddings celebrated in your family?)*
If your student struggles to find similarities and differences in how people celebrate weddings in different cultures, assist them by relating the question to their own life. For example, ask your student to identify similar toys, clothes, or books that they may have. Then ask your student to explain what makes the items in each category similar. As you discuss the similarities with your student, encourage them to identify differences among items in each category. For example, your student may say they have striped shirts that have similar colors or patterns. Your student may then assess that they are different because they're from unlike brands or have different lengths. Additionally, answers to the last question may vary. Ensure that your student provides some examples of how weddings are celebrated in their family. If they are unsure, encourage them to ask a parent or relative.

Learning Styles

Auditory learners may enjoy creating a podcast about their culture. They can include details about their language, traditional foods, and clothes, and holidays that they celebrate.

Visual learners may enjoy making a slideshow showing the different ways people celebrate holidays around the world. They can include different holidays and also different traditions from different cultures for the same holiday.

Kinesthetic learners may enjoy creating a sculpture with modeling clay of an object that is important in their culture. After they build their model, they can explain what this object is and how it is important to their culture.

LESSON 40
How Are Cultures Alike and Different?

Extension Activities

Comparing and Contrasting Cultural Folktales
Have your student research famous children's folktales from around the world by using an online search engine. Encourage your student to select at least two folktales by retrieving online texts or videos. Then have your student compare and contrast these cultural folktales, including notable features from the story, moral of the story, and how they represent their country or region's culture. Be sure to compare and contrast each folktale to your student's own culture. For example, *Momotaro* is a famous children's folktale in Japan. It tells the story of a boy who recruited a group of animals to fight monsters that were ravaging the town. The story is important, because Momotaro, the featured character, fought to protect his elder parents and citizens in town. Honoring one's family and society are seen as noble features in Japan. Additionally, peaches, known as "*momo*," are a staple fruit of the country. Other cultural folktales to consider are *The Wolf Queen* (Africa), *The King With Horse's Ears* (Europe), and *The Bird Sweet Magic* (South America).

Fashion World Showcase
With your student, create a fashion world showcase of different cultures around the world by making paper dolls. First, have your student research traditional outfits from at least five different countries or regions around the world, including the United States. On a separate piece of paper, ask your student to draw clothing that both men and women wear. Then have your student cut out their drawings and categorize them based on their country or region. As your student completes this activity, encourage them to think about the similarities and differences of clothing between men and women, from country to country or region to region, and to their own lives. To promote deeper thinking, ask your student to think about how cultural differences can create stereotypes and discuss why they can be harmful to people.

Answer Key

Explore *(Look at the images of what Santa looks like in the United States and United Kingdom. What are some of their similarities and differences?)*
Answers will vary. Possible answers: They both have long white beards, are wearing white gloves, and are wearing big coats. One is wearing all red and has a sack of toys. The other one is wearing a light blue coat and has a fancy hat or headdress.

Take a Closer Look
Answers will vary, but they should reflect your student's own culture and traditions.

Write *(How do you celebrate the New Year?)*
Answers will vary. Possible answers: Ensure your student writes examples of how they celebrate the New Year.

Write *(How are wedding celebrations similar and different around the world? How are weddings celebrated in your family?)*
Answers will vary. Possible answers: People wear special clothes or special colors, and they have special wedding ceremonies. In America, brides wear white dresses, but in India, the bride wears red clothing and lots of jewelry. In China and Taiwan, the bride wears red and the groom might, too. In the Congo, the bride and groom can't smile on their wedding day because they need to show that they take their marriage seriously.

Practice

LESSON 40
How Are Cultures Alike and Different?

Aspects of Culture	Similarities	Differences	Drawing
Holiday Celebrations	spending time with friends and family; counting down to midnight	Japan: people eat noodles called soba; monks ring bells Turkey: people sprinkle salt on their doorsteps Denmark: people break plates	varies
Wedding Celebrations	having a wedding ceremony and reception	India: brides wear red and lots of jewelry China: brides (and sometimes the groom) wear red Congo: brides and grooms are not allowed to smile	varies

Show What You Know
1. A and B
2. A
3. C
4. ceremony
5. red
6. Answers will vary. The answer should reflect what your student eats for breakfast.
7. Answers will vary. The answer should reflect your student's style of clothing and/or the traditional style of clothing for their country.

LESSON 41
When Cultures Meet

Lesson Objectives

By the end of this lesson, your student will be able to:

- describe ways that different cultures interact or influence each other
- identify how people can travel in a community and the world
- describe reasons why people might migrate to a different area or country

Supporting Your Student

Explore
As your student reads about the Hagia Sophia, it may be helpful to search for videos by using an online search engine. Have your student focus on the history of the famous monument. This includes why the Hagia Sophia was built, who built the Hagia Sophia, who the Byzantines and Ottomans were, and unique features of the monument. These questions can help your student understand the influence of the Hagia Sophia on people in society, including the structure being the most important building in the Eastern Christian world for more than nine hundred years.

Read *(Cultural Interaction and Influence)*
As your student reads through this section, it may be helpful to relate how different cultures interact or influence your student's life. For example, if your student speaks a different language, ask them when they speak the language, who they speak the language with, and why they speak the language. These are examples of cultural interaction. To help your student understand how language influences their life, ask them if they practice customs or traditions from a specific culture. If your student does not speak another language, consider the cultural foods they may like to eat, such as pasta, chicken tandori, or sushi. Then proceed to discuss with your student how these foods create cultural interaction or influence their life.

Learning Styles

Auditory learners may enjoy interviewing a person who has migrated to or from another country. This can include a friend or family member. Your student could ask questions about their positive experiences as well as the difficulties they had along their travels.

Visual learners may enjoy watching documentaries about traveling to different countries. Ask them how learning about other countries and their cultures influences them. What things about that country do they find interesting?

Kinesthetic learners may enjoy learning basic words and phrases from a romance language, such as French, Spanish, Italian, Portuguese, Romanian, and Catalan. Encourage your student to write a short poem using the words that they learned!

Extension Activities

Migration Stories and Opinion Column
If your student enjoys reading, retrieve animated books about human migration from your local bookstore or library. Recommended books include *The Arabic Quilt: An Immigrant Story* by Aya Khalil, which is a story about a little girl's journey from Egypt to America. *Wherever I Go* by Mary Wagley Copp tells the story of a little girl living in a refugee camp in Africa. *A Journey Toward Hope* by Victor Hinojosa is a story about migrant children traveling together from Mexico to the border of the United States. Have your student read independently or read aloud to them. Then, discuss with your student the major themes and elements of each story. To deepen student inquiry, encourage your student to write an opinion piece after reading. Ask your student to write what the story is about, what they learned from it, and why other people should read it.

LESSON 41
When Cultures Meet

Cultural Influences in Music
If your student enjoys music, have your student research the origins of different music genres, such as jazz, pop, rap, or country by using an online search engine. Ask your student to examine how different cultures have influenced the creation of the music genre, how music has spread, and how it has affected people in society. For example, while jazz was developed in the United States, it was strongly influenced by African and European music styles. African music centers on drumming, which has influenced the drumming styles in jazz. The saxophone and piano, which are popular instruments used in jazz, come from Europe. Additionally, jazz's influences on American culture are massive, influencing fashion and poetry in the 1920s to the Civil Rights movement in the 1950s and 1960s.

Answer Key

Explore
Ensure your student circles features that are unique to Christianity (mosaics) and Islam (Arabic murals and minarets).

Write (Why do people travel or migrate?)
Answers will vary. Possible answers: People may travel for fun, to visit family and friends, to study, or for work. People may migrate to look for better jobs, to find less expensive places to live, to escape persecution, or flee natural disasters like floods.

Practice
Answers will vary. Possible answers:

Show What You Know
1. interact
2. influence
3. migrate
4. jobs
5. natural
6. adapt
7. Latin
8. Answers will vary. Possible answers: Food can be influenced by different cultures when people learn how to make dishes from different cultures, like pizza. People can then adjust the toppings or ingredients used in pizza to reflect their own culture.
9. Answers will vary. Possible answers: car, bus, boat, or airplane.

LESSON 42
How Immigrants Help Their Communities

Lesson Objectives

By the end of this lesson, your student will be able to:
- explain how communities can benefit from immigrants
- identify an example of how immigrants have contributed to your community

Supporting Your Student

Explore *(Migration Reasons)*
You may want to help your student by discussing reasons why people move. You might be able to give an example of someone your student knows who moved. It could be a good friend of the family or a classmate. Discuss reasons why families move. Some move to be closer to family, for a new job in another city, or for better climate. This may help your student with this activity.

Write *(How might foods from other countries benefit a community?)*
If your student is not familiar with restaurants and stores that sell food and other products from other countries in your community, a field trip might be helpful. You could research online to find businesses or restaurants that sell food and other products from other countries.

Practice *(Immigrant Benefits)*
Your student may benefit from first discussing what they see in each picture. Then you could ask and discuss how the community benefits from what is happening in this picture.

Learning Styles

Auditory learners may enjoy listening to immigrant students telling their stories on podcasts.

Visual learners may enjoy taking photographs and making a collage of images that show immigrants contributing to their community.

Kinesthetic learners may enjoy going on a community field trip to find out more about the stores or restaurants that immigrants run.

Extension Activities

Immigration Puppet Show
Have your student first research their community's history to discover who the founder or founders were and whether they were immigrants. If they were immigrants, your student could find out which country or countries they were from and learn more about their contributions to the community. Your student could then create a puppet show showing how their community was discovered and the contributions they learned that were provided to their community.

Cultural Festival
Find and attend some cultural festivals in your community where your student can learn more about the food and culture of the immigrants that live in your community and/or their own cultural heritage.

LESSON 42
How Immigrants Help Their Communities

Answer Key

Explore
Answers will vary. Possible answer: People move to different countries or other areas because the mom or dad gets a new job with another company. Then they must move to the place where the new job is at. Also, people move to other areas because the climate where they live is very cold. This causes them to move to warmer areas.

Write *(How might foods from other countries benefit a community?')*
Answers will vary. Possible answer: The benefits of restaurants and stores selling food and other products from other countries are that you can learn about new foods and products. You can also share those new foods and products with your friends.

Practice *(Immigrant Benefits)*
Answers will vary. Possible answer:

1. The community could eat new types of food when immigrants open new restaurants.
2. Immigrants could be scientists and doctors who help the community by creating new medicines and treating people who are ill.
3. People in the community can listen to new types of music.
4. People can also learn a new language from immigrants.

Show What You Know
5. False
6. False
7. True
8. True
9. True
10. True
11. True
12. False

LESSON 43
Chapter 5 Review

Lesson Objectives

By the end of this lesson, your student will review the following big ideas from Chapter 5.

- People show their culture in the way they live, with their ideas, and with their beliefs. (Lesson 39)
- There are differences and similarities when you compare the world's many cultures with their food, dance, music, celebrations, and traditions. (Lesson 40)
- Cultures influence each other when they interact through music, sports, languages, and travel. (Lesson 41)
- Immigrants can help their communities by their jobs, food, and products that they bring to the communities. (Lesson 42)

Supporting Your Student

Practice *(Vocabulary Activity)*
If your student has difficulty choosing between the two vocabulary words, you can prompt them to say the sentence aloud using each word and ask themselves, "Does this sound right? Does it make sense?" You can discuss the meaning of the sentence and the meanings of the words before your student selects the word.

Practice *(People From Different Cultures Are Alike and Different)*
If your student has difficulty coming up with similarities and differences when comparing their culture with Maria's culture, you can prompt them by asking questions that pertain to Maria's culture.

- Do you speak Spanish?
- Do you celebrate a holiday on September 15th?
- Do you eat mangoes?

Practice *(Immigrants Can Help Their Communities)*
Your student can find ideas of the different ways that immigrants help their communities in Lesson 42. They can also use examples they find in their own communities of immigrants working in different professions, owning businesses including restaurants and stores, and volunteering in different ways in the community. Your student may want to reread the reading sections from Lesson 42 and discuss them with you.

Learning Styles

Auditory learners may enjoy listening to books about people from other cultures. You can find lists of the top multicultural books for second grade. Search online for "multicultural books" and "second grade."

Visual learners may enjoy looking at the illustrations in different multicultural picture books and comparing the different cultures in the books. Your student could discuss the differences with you.

Kinesthetic learners may enjoy visiting an art museum where they can walk around as they explore the art from different cultures.

Extension Activities

LESSON 43
Chapter 5 Review

My Family Traditions Collage
Traditions are an important part of culture. Ask your student to create a collage describing the different traditions in their family. This can include ways they celebrate different holidays and special days, places they like to visit, and activities they enjoy doing together. It can also include family traditions that have been passed down from their ancestors.

Young Immigrants
Your student can search online for stories of young immigrants that tell about their stories of immigration and talk about the culture in their homelands. They can read their stories and watch their videos. Then they can discuss their findings with you.

My Heritage
Your student can research the history of their family to find out where their ancestors came from and find out more about the culture of their ancestors. Then, with your assistance, they can make a family tree.

Answer Key

Write *(How do people show their culture? List three ways and then describe what they do.)*
Possible answers: People show their culture through their food, clothing, traditions, and music. People eat different types of food. They may have traditions like celebrating certain holidays. They also listen to different types of music and play different musical instruments.

Write *(How do people learn about different cultures?)*
Possible answers: People learn about different cultures from the immigrants who live in their community. Immigrants open new businesses and restaurants. Then the people of the community can try their food and buy their products.

Practice *(Vocabulary Activity)*
1. cultures
2. adapt
3. migrate
4. language
5. interact
6. traditions
7. interact

Practice *(People from Different Cultures are Alike and Different)*
Possible answers: Similarities—celebrates Christmas and Easter, favorite fruit is mango, likes to play with dolls and ride a bike; Differences—speaking Spanish, calls soccer "fûtbol," celebrates the independence of my country on September 15

Practice *(Immigrants Help their Communities)*
Possible answers: Language: teaches their own language to other people in the community; Food: open a restaurant and serve food from their country; Art/music: play different musical instruments; Skills and Abilities: introduce new medicine to the community

CHAPTER 5
Assessment

Quick Review

Refer to the statement your student circled in the Show What You Know section to self-assess their knowledge of the chapter concepts. Then to assist in determining if your student is ready to take the assessment, consider:

- Having your student explain what culture is in their own words.
- Having your student give examples of different ways people show their culture.
- Having your student identify similarities and differences when comparing two cultures.
- Having your student give examples of different ways that cultures influence each other.
- Having your student give examples of the reasons people migrate.
- Having your student give examples of ways that immigrants help their communities.

CHAPTER 5
Assessment

Chapter Assessment

Project: Study an Immigrant Community

Project Requirements or Steps: For this project, teach a lesson based on the topics of this unit.

1. Have your student pick a community of immigrants to study. This could include grandparents or other relatives, or someone living on your block.

2. The student should interview an immigrant to prepare a summary on this immigrant community. Questions can include: "Where did you come from originally?" "How many people in your family came with you?" "What were some of the difficulties you encountered while moving here?" and "Can you share some of your culture and traditions that you feel you want to keep alive even though you have moved to a new community?"

3. The student should provide one of the following for assessment:

   - a summary of interview with immigrant
   - a poster of this immigrant's culture and traditions
   - a reflection of this immigrant moving to America and how they felt, how their life changed, and what customs/traditions they kept

4. The student assessment should be based on meeting criteria of all questions and thoroughness of answers. Your student's progress on this type of assessment will indicate whether or not to review previous chapters before going forward to the next chapter.

CHAPTER 5
Assessment

Chapter Assessment Rubric

Use the following rubric to grade your student's assessment.

	4	3	2	1	Points
Connection to the Chapter	The topic is clearly related to the chapter, and your student has information or discussion points that go above and beyond the information provided in the chapter.	The topic is clearly related to the chapter.	The topic is somewhat related to the chapter.	The topic is not related to the chapter.	
Questions	The questions asked by the interviewer are related to the topic and have significant depth.	The questions asked by the interviewer are on topic, but they do not necessarily further the conversation.	The questions asked by the interviewer start out on track but fall off topic.	The questions asked by the interviewer are completely off topic.	
Preparation	The student is well-prepared for the interview and conducts it in a professional manner.	The student is prepared for the interview and conducts it in a professional manner.	The student is not very well-prepared for the interview.	The student is not prepared for the interview.	
Clarification Questions	The student is able to effectively clarify any questions during the interview in an efficient manner.	The student is able to clarify most of the questions during the interview.	The student struggles to clarify the questions during the interview.	The student is unable to clarify any questions during the interview.	

Total Points _____/16

Average _____

CHAPTER 5
Assessment

Alternative Assessment

Fill in the blank with the correct word from the word bank.

Word Bank: adapt   culture   doctors   food immigrants   interact   job   migrate

1. _____ is the way people live, their ideas, and their beliefs.
2. Immigrants open restaurants and show their culture by selling their _____.
3. When people from different cultures get together and _____, they learn from each other.
4. Sometimes, people have to _____ or move to a different country.
5. People who move to a different country are called _____.
6. Immigrants have to _____ or change to fit the culture of their new country.
7. Immigrants help their community by becoming _____ who help sick people get well.
8. People migrate to other countries because of new _____ opportunities in the new country.

Look at the picture of a family eating in China.

9. How is this culture similar or different from your culture?

....
....
....
....
....

CHAPTER 5
Assessment

Alternative Assessment Answer Key

1. culture
2. food
3. interact
4. migrate
5. immigrants
6. adapt
7. doctors
8. job
9. Answers will vary. Possible answer: This culture is different from my culture because I eat with a fork and spoon. I do not eat with chopsticks.

LESSON 44
Communities Change Over Time

Lesson Objectives

By the end of this lesson, your student will be able to:
- explain ways communities can grow and change over time
- compare how your community has changed from the past to today

Supporting Your Student

Explore
As your student compares the two images, you may want to point out the details in each photograph. For instance, you may want to ask about the chairs in the modern picture and why those chairs are there. Then ask what forms of transportation are seen in the picture.

Read *(People Change Their Communities)*
Encourage your student to make connections to what they have learned about culture and community. You can ask them, "Do you think the changes in communication and transportation make it easier for different cultures to interact and influence each other? How can cultural influences change communities?"

Practice
It could be helpful for your student to do some online research for photographs from their own community so they can observe the houses, communication, and transportation in their community today. They can also ask relatives or friends to share photographs with them about their community.

Learning Styles

Auditory learners may enjoy listening to recordings of radio shows from the past and comparing those to the ways people entertain themselves today.

Visual learners may enjoy watching videos that show the changes that have happened in different cities over long periods of time.

Kinesthetic learners may enjoy going on a field trip in their community to find buildings from the past and comparing them to more modern buildings.

Extension Activities

Fashion Over Time
Your student can research how fashion and clothing in their community have changed over time. They can research online to find photographs or illustrations to see these changes. Your student can create a poster showing the progression of how fashion has changed over time and present it to their family.

Changes in Technology
Your student can choose one item to research in depth and discover how it has changed over time. For example, they can research how cars, computers, telephones, or televisions have changed over the years.

LESSON 44
Communities Change Over Time

Answer Key

Explore
Answers will vary. Possible answer: I notice that there are old cars in the older picture. One difference is that there are no cars in the newer picture, so people must walk now. There are chairs outside one building in the newer picture, unlike in the older picture.

Practice
Answers will vary. Possible answers:

Houses—The picture will show more houses in a neighborhood.

Communication—The picture will show cell phones.

Transportation—The picture will show cars on roads.

Weather—The picture will show thunderstorms and flooding.

Show What You Know
1. earthquake
2. technology
3. hurricane
4. transport
5. communicate
6. Answers will vary. Possible answer: My community has changed because it has many more houses.
7. Answers will vary. Possible answer: More cars are on the roads since my community was built.
8. Answers will vary. Possible answer: People use cell phones instead of mailing letters in my community.

LESSON 45
Conflicts and Cooperation Can Change Communities

Lesson Objectives
By the end of this lesson, your student will be able to:
- describe how conflict and cooperation can change a community
- describe how people and events caused change in your community

Supporting Your Student

Online Connection
Talk about the video *How Kids Can be Activists To Make Their Communities Better*, and discuss what is the best way to be an activist in your community. Ask your student: "What do you think our neighborhood needs help with?," "What could we do to improve this?," and "How would we go about doing this project?"

Explore
Watch the video with your student, *Handling Everyday Conflicts*, and stop often to discuss how the children are working out their everyday conflicts or disagreements. Whenever possible relate it to something that has happened in your community where people have had to work together to resolve an issue. Emphasize how as adults you continue to work out issues with others so that there is less conflict in a community.

Read *(Conflicts and Cooperation)*
Some examples of conflicts that have changed communities are provided. You can support your student by discussing examples of conflicts that have changed their community. Go online and look at some news articles of community events such as hurricanes, unemployment, or other events that had an impact on the community you live in. Some examples of countries and people cooperating to change their communities are provided. You can support your student by discussing examples of cooperation in their community. Ask your student for suggestions on how to cooperate with others. Talk about how they get along with friends when having a playdate or choosing a game to play.

Write *(What are some events that have changed your community? Have there been any conflicts, natural disasters, or other events that changed your community?)*
Be prepared with examples of a conflict or sudden change in your community that caused unrest and caused people to react differently. Talk about what kinds of events can make people overreact and cause conflict in the community. Think of something that happened in your own community that your student experienced and ask, "How do you think that could have been handled differently?"

Learning Styles
Auditory learners may enjoy having a discussion about how problems in their community can be solved. Your student can pick a particular problem they are interested in and brainstorm ways to solve that problem.

Visual learners may enjoy illustrating some of the changes that have happened in their community.

Kinesthetic learners may enjoy volunteering in their community to create positive changes.

Extension Activities

Volunteering in the Community
Your student can research local opportunities to help in their community. They can cooperate with local organizations working to change their community in a positive way. You can also help your student organize a volunteer project, like helping a neighbor carry groceries or cleaning up the local park.

Go to Local Library
Your student can visit the local library to learn about free courses and events they schedule for the community. Discuss with your student the importance of each of these types of activities. Look at opportunities for seniors, parents, and children. Discuss why each segment of the community would benefit from these resources/programs at the library.

LESSON 45
Conflicts and Cooperation Can Change Communities

Answer Key

Write *(What is an example of a conflict in your community? What is an example of something that makes you feel safe in your community?)*
Answers will vary. Possible answers: conflicts—hurricanes, road collapsing, virus, property lines; safety—firefighters, police officers, government workers, school workers, parents, activist organizations, volunteers

Write *(What is an example of people cooperating or working together to change their community?)*
Answers will vary. Possible answers: working in community gardens, building houses for people in need, volunteering, walking someone's dog, babysitting, helping with chores

Write *(What are some events that have changed your community? Have there been any conflicts, natural disasters, or other events that changed your community?)*
Answers will vary. Possible answers: a community affected by a hurricane, a family affected by a fire, flooding

Show What You Know
1. B
2. A
3. Answers will vary. Possible answers: natural disasters, virus outbreaks, elections
4. Answers will vary. Possible answers: working together in government offices, schools, fire stations, police stations

LESSON 46
Changes in Your Community on a Timeline

Lesson Objectives

By the end of this lesson, your student will be able to:

- create a timeline for your community to show change from the past to the present

Supporting Your Student

Explore

It might be helpful to gather some books about the history of your community that will provide your student with the necessary information specific to their community. Find out if there are local museums you can visit with your student to learn more about their community. If you can, find people in the community who can share relevant information with your student. Additionally, you can search online for current articles about events happening in your community and point out any information that shows the change in your community.

Read *(What Is a Timeline?)*

Encourage your student to keep sticky notes available while they read the examples of the ways that communities change. They can write down examples that come to mind that are specific to their community. They will be able to use these sticky notes when they complete the practice activity. You can print out some pictures they find that they can incorporate into their timeline.

Practice

It might be helpful for your student to have photographs available to add to their timeline. If they do not have photographs, they can add their own illustrations. Your student can complete the timeline in the textbook or use an online tool to create their timeline. They can also create a large timeline outdoors. You can decide with your student the best way to create the timeline. The timeline in the textbook can serve as a draft for a larger, more detailed project. Your student may even be able to create their timeline in a Google Slides or PowerPoint format.

Learning Styles

Auditory learners may enjoy giving an oral presentation of the timeline in their community where they explain to other people each step in the timeline.

Visual learners may enjoy finding photographs or other illustrations to add to the timeline of their community.

Kinesthetic learners may enjoy creating their timeline on a sidewalk and inviting other people to walk the timeline with them and learn about their community.

Extension Activities

Local Museum

Go on a field trip to a local museum with your student so they learn more about the history of their community, its important events, and the changes that have happened. Have your student take notes and create a brochure for someone who is thinking about visiting their community.

Sharing the Timeline With an Audience

Find an opportunity for your student to share their timeline with other people in the community in some way. Your student could present the timeline to friends, neighbors, or family members. Or perhaps your student could post an interactive timeline online for people from the community to comment and add additional details.

LESSON 46
Changes in Your Community on a Timeline

Answer Key
Practice
Answers will vary.

Show What You Know
1. timeline
2. community
3. events
4. People

LESSON 47
Community Changes From the Past to Present

Lesson Objectives
By the end of this lesson, your student will be able to:
- compare and contrast how a community from another part of the world has changed from the past to today

Supporting Your Student

Explore
To assist your student, refer your student to the sidebar on page 4. Your student will find some photos of what life was like 100 years ago. You may want to discuss these photos with your student. Also, you could find other photos online or have your student look for more photos of what life was like 100 years ago.

Read (People and Jobs)
Population has increased greatly in the past 100 years all over the world. You may want to discuss that the world population today is almost 8 billion people. In 1900, the population of the world was 1.5 billion. You may want to discuss how medicine and technology has helped grow our population. It allows people to live longer lives.

Write (Describe two changes in communities in China from 100 years ago to today.)
You may want to discuss with your student the possibilities for this question. You may want to ask your student what they learned after reading about hobbies, homes, education, and people. These have changed from past to present.

Practice
Ask your student to discuss first the transportation, jobs, and types of homes today. Ask what job and transportation people they know have. For the government section, ask about your country's leader. Does your country have a president, prime minister, king, queen, or someone else?

Learning Styles

Auditory learners may enjoy watching a video about Chinese communities from long ago. They would enjoy hearing about the things that the Chinese people did many years ago as well as seeing those things.

Visual learners may enjoy making a collage of past and present images from China or from their own community.

Kinesthetic learners may enjoy acting out a skit about a community in the past and today. Keep in mind they should include the major categories from the Read section.

Extension Activities

Office or Farm?
Find pictures of objects or tasks that people are doing on a farm and pictures of objects or tasks that people are doing in an office today. Have your student look at each picture and sort them based on whether they took place on a farm or in an office. Ask your student whether the pictures of the objects or tasks for the farm could take place today. Some might and some might not. Then do the same for the office pictures.

Elderly Family Member Discussion
Find an elderly family member or neighbor. Have your student discuss what life was like many years ago when they were a child. How did they get to school? What jobs did their parents do? What did they like to do in their spare time? Also, ask if they have any pictures to show your student.

LESSON 47
Community Changes From the Past to Present

Answer Key

Explore

Answers will vary. Possible answer: Life would be very different. I would not be able to play video games, but I would probably be playing outside more with my brothers and sisters. I would have to walk to school, but school would probably be closer. I would probably read more too.

Write *(Describe two changes in communities in China from 100 years ago to today.)*

Answers will vary. Possible answer: Two changes in the communities in China are their homes and hobbies. People used to live in small houses in China in the past, but today many of them live in tall apartment buildings. Another change is their hobbies. They played outside more in the past, but today they play video games and watch television.

Practice

Answers will vary. Possible answers:

Transportation Past: horse and buggy

Transportation Today: car

Jobs Past: farmers

Jobs Today: computer programmer

Homes Past: small houses

Homes Today: apartment buildings

Government Past: one leader over the whole country

Government Today: one leader over the whole country

Show What You Know
1. False
2. True
3. True
4. True
5. False
6. False
7. True

LESSON 48
Community Conflict and Cooperation

Lesson Objectives
By the end of this lesson, your student will be able to:
- describe how conflict and cooperation have shaped the community over time
- explore how people and events caused change in the community

Supporting Your Student

Explore
Look at the picture. Discuss what you see in the picture with your student. You see that the children are on a couch, and there is a remote next to one of them. Ask your student what the two children could have been upset about.

Read (Conflict)
With the information about identity theft, discuss what happens when someone loses their identity. Explain that people who get their identity stolen means that someone is pretending to be that person in order to use their credit cards or bank accounts. They are stealing their money.

Write (Think about a time where you cooperated to help solve a problem. What did you do?)
You may want to ask your student about a time when they saw a problem and figured out a way to help. Then have them tell you about it. Ask them what they did to help.

Practice
One way to help your student with this activity is to discuss each statement. Ask your student if that person is helping or hurting someone. Usually, if they are helping someone, then it is a cooperation. If they are hurting someone, then it is a conflict.

Learning Styles

Auditory learners may enjoy interviewing a friend or family member about a conflict that they had with someone and how they resolved a conflict.

Visual learners may enjoy reading a book about conflict and cooperation. One suggestion is the book *Hudson and Tallulah Take Sides* by Anna King and Christopher Weyant. They may enjoy discussing conflict and cooperation from the book with their instructor.

Kinesthetic learners may enjoy going to a nonprofit organization and helping out. They may want to think about the ways they are helping their community.

Extension Activities

Community Memory Game
Have your student create a memory game with cards. Half of the cards should have a different job on them. Their matching card should be someone or something specific that it helps. For example, one job could be a teacher. The matching card would be students.

Create a Book
Have your student write and illustrate their own book. It should be about how cooperation has shaped their community. Your student may need to research how their community has helped others over the years. Help your student write the story. Your student can illustrate the pages.

LESSON 48
Community Conflict and Cooperation

Answer Key

Explore
Answers will vary. Possible answer: The children are brother and sister. They are on the couch with a remote control there. So there was probably a conflict between them about watching television. One wanted to watch a certain show, and the other one wanted to watch something different. Their parents resolved the conflict, but the children are still upset.

Write *(Think about a time where you cooperated to help solve a problem. What did you do?)*
Answers will vary. Possible answer: I saw trash on my street and decided to pick up all the trash that I saw.

Practice
1. cooperation
2. conflict
3. conflict
4. cooperation
5. conflict
6. cooperation

Show What You Know
7. safes
8. technology
9. identity
10. city
11. neighbors
12. nonprofit organizations
13. police

LESSON 49
Timeline for the Community

Lesson Objectives
By the end of this lesson, your student will be able to:
- create a timeline for this community to show change from the past to the present

Supporting Your Student

Explore
You may want to discuss with your student about the games and activities that children did to have fun on a farm, especially in 1900. You may want to research online games and things that children in 1900 did for fun.

Read *(The Community in the 1960s)*
There are several types of transportation, hobbies, and jobs that existed in the 1960s that still exist today. You may need to differentiate the ways in which these things were used back then and today. For example, you may want to explain that there were airplanes in the 1960s, but it cost so much money to fly that many families could not afford it. Therefore, there were not as many flights back then as there are today.

Write *(What did many people in the community do for jobs? How did they travel?)*
Remind your student that there was very little technology available during the 1900s. You may want to have your student research if they would like to learn about the other jobs available during this time.

Practice
To help your student, you may want your student to look back at the reading and identify certain things that fit into those categories during that time period. Then you can help them think of what they could draw for each picture.

Learning Styles

Auditory learners may enjoy interviewing a grandparent and asking them what their community was like when they were young. Your student could also ask their parents what hobbies they did for fun when they were young.

Visual learners may enjoy creating a scene from the 1900s, 1960s, or today using craft supplies.

Kinesthetic learners may enjoy acting out a story for you or family members based on the stories they wrote about the different time periods.

Extension Activities

Create Your Own Timeline
Research online for more types of transportation, education, and jobs that have developed in your community within the past 100 years. Then create a timeline using that information. You may need to help your student with the research and creation of the timeline.

How Communities Were Built
Read about how communities were built. A good book to check out would be *Look Where We Live!: A First Book of Community Building* by Scot Ritchie. Then have your student discuss with you what they learned about how communities are built.

LESSON 49
Timeline for the Community

Answer Key

Explore

Answers will vary. Possible answers: I would like to live here because there are a lot of things to do. I could play games with my brothers and sisters. I could also play with the animals on the farm.

Write *(What did many people in the community do for jobs? How did they travel?)*

Many people in the community were farmers. These are the jobs that they did. They traveled mostly by walking or riding horses.

Practice

Answers will vary. Possible answers:

- Transportation in 1900: They could include a person walking, riding a horse, or riding in a horse and buggy.
- Jobs in 1960: This could be either a teacher, dentist, secretary, store worker, or another job from the 1960s.
- Education today: This may include technology or computers. It could also include many students in a classroom.
- Technology/tools in 1900: This could include a plow or hammer.

Show What You Know

1. farms
2. horses
3. cars
4. computers
5. airplanes

LESSON 50
How Communities Have Changed

Lesson Objectives

By the end of this lesson, your student will be able to:
- compare and contrast how communities have changed over time

Supporting Your Student

Explore
One way to help your student is to drive or walk around your community and point out some of the changes that have taken place. For instance, you could point to a building and say, "That was built recently," or, "This was all farmland until they built these buildings."

Read (Differences Between Communities)
You may want to discuss how subways can be found in major US cities. You can show your student a map of the subway systems in the United States compared to China's subway system. Prompt your student to use words like "bigger," "smaller," "more," and "less" to compare and contrast the subway system in both countries.

Write (What changes are the same in both communities?)
If your student is struggling with finding the changes that were the same, you may want to reread the first section together. Then discuss the similarities of each topic in that first section, such as how the jobs, transportation, and education are the same in both communities.

Practice
One way to help with this activity is to refer to the second section of the reading. Then discuss the ways in which the Chinese community is different from the US community.

Learning Styles

Auditory learners may enjoy watching a video about Chinese communities in the past and today.

Visual learners may enjoy creating a Venn diagram about the differences and similarities between the communities in China and the United States.

Kinesthetic learners may enjoy acting out the skit created from the extension activity.

Extension Activities

Bingo
Create a few bingo cards. Write "United States and China" at the top of the cards. Then have your student write various items in each column from the sections on transportation, jobs, education, and hobbies. List the items in the correct column for either the United States or China. Write the list of items on a sheet of paper. Play the bingo game. Read an item. Then mark it off your card and have your student mark it off their card. The first card to have five in a row wins.

Recreate a Scene
Have your student create a scene of a community from China or the United States as if they were going to take a picture of it. Create the scene using different props and backgrounds. Then take a picture of it.

LESSON 50
How Communities Have Changed

Answer Key

Explore
Answers will vary. Possible answers: The community has grown bigger or smaller. More buildings were built. More cars and buses are on the street.

Write *(What changes are the same in both communities?)*
Answers will vary. Possible answers: Both communities have some of the same changes. They both have technical jobs like computer engineers and data scientists. They both use cars as transportation. They both have more people going to school.

Practice
1. B
2. A
3. A

Show What You Know
4. True
5. False
6. True
7. True
8. True
9. False
10. False
11. True
12. False

LESSON 51
Chapter 6 Review

Lesson Objectives

By the end of this lesson, your student will review the following big ideas from Chapter 6.

- Communities change and grow over time. (Lesson 44)
- Conflict and cooperation can change a community. (Lesson 45)
- People and events cause change in your community. (Lesson 46)
- A community can change from the past to the present. (Lesson 47)
- There can be similar and different changes occurring in communities' histories. (Lesson 48)
- A timeline can show the changes in your community from past to present. (Lesson 49)
- Changes in a community can be based on its transportation, education, jobs, and hobbies. (Lesson 50)

Supporting Your Student

Write *(Describe how communities change. What happens to them?)*
You may want to help your student by discussing ways conflicts took place in communities. Then have your student discuss ways in which the community changed from the conflicts. You can also help your student describe ways that the communities cooperated. Then ask them about the changes that happened through that cooperation.

Practice *(Crossword Puzzle)*
If your student is struggling with the crossword puzzle, you may want to quiz your student over the chapter's vocabulary. Go back through the vocabulary words and provide the definitions. See if they can give the vocabulary word, or provide the word and see if they can provide the definition. See if that practice helps them do the crossword puzzle.

Practice *(Job Chart)*
Your student may have a problem with certain jobs, such as mechanics, secretaries, and store workers. Obviously some of these existed in 1900, and all of them exist now. However, the activity is wanting the student to place the jobs where they happened mostly compared to other jobs.

Learning Styles

Auditory learners may enjoy listening to or watching a movie about common jobs in the 1960s. This also may be helpful in determining which jobs were the most common within this time.

Visual learners may enjoy going through a museum in person or online to see conflicts and cooperation experienced by a community.

Kinesthetic learners may enjoy attending a reenactment of a battle at a community history day either in your own community or another community that has a strong history.

Extension Activities

My Timeline
To practice making timelines, your student may want to make a timeline of their own life. Have them think of important events in their own life and write them down. Then create a timeline on a white piece of paper. Write each date and event description in the order it happened. They could also draw and color a picture of each event on the timeline.

Community Diorama
A diorama is a scene in a box with a hole cut into the top and side. You look through the side of the box to see the scene. In this activity, have your student create a scene that depicts a main difference that took place in their community from the past to the present.

Answer Key

Write *(Describe how communities change. What happens to them?)*

LESSON 51
Chapter 6 Review

Answers will vary. Possible answers: Communities change because of conflict and cooperation. Natural disasters such as earthquakes and hurricanes can cause people to move away. They can also get people to cooperate. Then nonprofit organizations could be established to help the citizens in the community. Technology could also change a community. That would create more technical jobs.

Write *(How have Chinese communities and American communities changed in different ways?)*
Answers will vary. Possible answers: Chinese and American communities have changed in different ways. First, Chinese communities have their grandparents live with their families, and American communities usually do not. Second, Chinese families often live in apartments, and American communities have more houses for their families.

Practice *(Crossword Puzzle)*
Across
- 2. volunteer
- 6. cooperation

Down
- 1. hurricane
- 3. technology
- 4. earthquake
- 5. conflict

Practice *(Matching)*
1. D
2. B
3. E
4. C
5. A

Practice *(Job Chart)*
1900s: blacksmiths, farmers

1960s: mechanics, secretaries, store workers

Today: computer engineers, data scientists, software developers

Note: Answers may vary. Discuss with your student that, even though we have some blacksmiths and farmers now, we have fewer than in the 1900s. We also still have mechanics, secretaries, and store workers, but more people did those jobs in the 1960s.

CHAPTER 6
Assessment

Quick Review

Refer to the statement your student circled in the Show What You Know section to self-assess their knowledge of the chapter concepts. Then to assist in determining if your student is ready to take the assessment, consider:

- Having your student discuss changes to communities over time based on natural disasters, cooperation, and conflict.
- Having your student name some changes that can be seen from the past to the present involving transportation, education, hobbies, and jobs.

CHAPTER 6
Assessment

Chapter Assessment

Project: Timeline

Project Requirements or Steps:

Create two timelines showing the similarities and differences between your community's changes and a Chinese community's changes. Identify the changes for each community and write those down. Then put those events in order for each timeline. Think about how the events are similar and different.

1. Write down the five changes (events) that have happened over time in your own community.
2. Number the events in the order they happened.
3. Draw a line across a piece of white paper. Then write the events in order above and below the line across the page.
4. Next write down the five changes (events) that have happened over time in the Chinese community.
5. Number the events in the order they happened.
6. Draw a line across another piece of white paper. Then write the events in order above and below the line across the page.
7. Look at the events on both timelines. Find the similarities and differences.
8. Write down two similarities and two differences.

CHAPTER 6
Assessment

Chapter Assessment Rubric

Use the following rubric to grade your student's assessment.

	4	3	2	1	Points
Connection to the Chapter	The timeline is clearly connected to the chapter.	The timeline is connected to the chapter.	The timeline is somewhat connected to the chapter.	The timeline is not connected to the chapter.	
Creativity	The timeline is very creative and aesthetically appealing.	The timeline is creative and aesthetically appealing.	The timeline is somewhat creative and aesthetically appealing.	The timeline is not creative or aesthetically appealing.	
Information	The information or data is accurate and easy to follow.	The information or data is accurate.	The information or data is somewhat accurate.	The information or data is not accurate.	
Grammar and Mechanics	There are no grammar and punctuation mistakes.	There are one or two grammar and punctuation mistakes.	There are several grammar and punctuation mistakes.	There are a distracting number of grammar and punctuation mistakes.	

Total Points _____/16

Average _____

Discover! SOCIAL STUDIES • GRADE 2 • CHAPTER 6 ASSESSMENT

CHAPTER 6
Assessment

Alternative Assessment

Circle the correct answer.

1. True or False — A community can grow by buildings being built and new things being created.

2. True or False — A community changes over time by changes in transportation and communication.

3. True or False — A conflict could change a community and make people feel safe.

4. True or False — People sometimes cooperate after a natural disaster by helping each other.

5. True or False — Cooperation with neighbors improves neighborhoods.

6. True or False — A Chinese community changed from riding cars in the past to riding horses today.

7. True or False — A main difference of a Chinese community from the past to today is the creation of a government.

8. True or False — Community conflict and crime have changed because of technology.

9. True or False — People can cooperate by volunteering in a community.

10. True or False — A timeline of the changes in your community would show the most recent event first.

11. How could a community change over time?
    A. natural disasters
    B. television
    C. animals
    D. books and magazines

12. What would be included in a timeline for your community to show changes?
    A. number of cities in your country
    B. weather and climate
    C. oceans and other bodies of water
    D. technology advancements

13. How has law enforcement changed in communities?
    A. Law enforcement has decreased over time.
    B. Police help the citizens of a community now.
    C. There are various types of law enforcement.
    D. Police have now become law enforcement.

14. Which of the following categories is a difference between changes in Chinese and American communities?
    A. education
    B. traditions
    C. hobbies
    D. types of jobs

CHAPTER 6
Assessment

Alternative Assessment Answer Key

1. True
2. True
3. False
4. True
5. True
6. False
7. False
8. True
9. True
10. False
11. A
12. D
13. C
14. B

LESSON 52
Indigenous People

Lesson Objectives

By the end of this lesson, your student will be able to:
- describe who Indigenous people are
- explain why culture is important to Indigenous people

Supporting Your Student

Take a Closer Look
In the past few years, more and more cities are making the change in order to honor the Indigenous people of the past and present. To help extend your student's understanding of indigenous stories you could find some other stories from various tribes online. Some story ideas are *The Little Boy Who Changed Into an Owl*, *Rainbow and the Autumn Leaves*, *The Fox and the Crows*, and *The Bee and the Fox* are all indigenous stories you could search online for. These stories are a glimpse into different cultures.

Read (Colonization)
Your student might not be familiar with the concept of colonization. Your student could benefit from a review of this vocabulary word. Also, examples of colonization in history will further support your student's understanding. One example that could be shared with your student is the English settlers at Jamestown, who colonized the Powhatans' land. English settlers took over the Indigenous people's land and changed their culture. This can be a challenge to teach as you want to make sure your student receives the information objectively. You can prompt your student by saying, "Why may the settlers have wanted or needed the land?" or "Do you think both groups could live there?" Giving your student the chance to see the perspective of the settlers and the Indigenous people while looking at real-world examples can help students connect meaning to a new concept.

Write (How did colonization affect the Indigenous people's culture?)
It might be helpful to create a cause and effect chart to offer a visual for your student. For example, the settlers came to America (have your student write or draw this), felt their culture was the right way to live. The settlers forced their own culture on the Indigenous people (have the learner write or draw this), and it affected the Indigenous people as they lost some of their customs, freedoms, rights, property and sacred practices.

Practice (Family Traditions)
Before starting, review the vocabulary; traditions, culture, and customs of your student's family. It would also be helpful to look at pictures of family traditions such as birthday parties. This will help the student come up with a family tradition to write and/or draw.

Learning Styles

Auditory learners may enjoy listening to audiobooks about various Indigenous tribes. They may also enjoy talking to an Indigenous person local to the area.

Visual learners may enjoy exploring the art of Indigenous peoples. They may also enjoy videos created by Indigenous people teaching about their culture.

Kinesthetic learners may enjoy playing a game of red light; to go on the green light, they will need to review a vocabulary word.

Extension Activities

Visit an Indigenous Site
Indigenous people can be found all around the world. Your area may be home to an Indigenous group. Do a quick online search of your area, and, if possible, visit a park, trail, or historic site that is part of the history of the Indigenous people in your area.

Art Creation
Have the student create an art piece inspired by their own family traditions and customs. This can be a drawing, painting, or mural with chalk. Have them visualize certain traditions and then create a piece of art from that visualization.

LESSON 52
Indigenous People

Answer Key

Explore *(What Indigenous tribe lives in Arizona?)*
Navajo Nation

Write *(What does culture mean?)*
Culture is a group's way of life, including things such as food, language, clothing, tools, art, or beliefs.

Write *(How did colonization affect the Indigenous people's culture?)*
Indigenous people were forced to unlearn their culture and learn the culture of the settlers.

Practice *(Family Traditions)*
Answers and drawings will vary. It should include a tradition practiced by your student.

Sidebar *(Online Connection)*
The research should answer the following questions regarding a local Indigenous group of people:
- What is their nation or tribe name?
- When did they first arrive in the area?
- What is a story they tell?
- What type of art do they create?

Show What You Know
1. B
2. C
3. A
4. C
5. True
6. False
7. True
8. Possible answers: Culture is important to Indigenous people because it connects them to their ancestors. Culture is important to Indigenous people because it helps them remember their traditions. Indigenous people don't want to lose their traditions, so their culture is important.

LESSON 53
Indigenous People in Your Area

Lesson Objectives

By the end of this lesson, your student will be able to:
- identify a tribe of Indigenous people in your region or area
- find where they lived on a map
- describe types of shelters and housing Indigenous people built

Supporting Your Student

Explore
It would be helpful to look at further examples of shelter to show your student that shelter can be made out of numerous resources. You can research traditional houses in the area you live in to show your student. Also, it might be helpful to walk around a neighborhood and look at the various houses; some are small, some have multiple levels, and they come in different colors. Ask your student what material the homes are made from. This will help connect the lesson to their life experience. When it is time for your student to draw their shelter, ask them what materials their home is made from? How is their home similar to the homes pictured in this section? How is their home different from the homes pictured in this section?

Read (All Around The World)
As your student reads these sections encourage them to stop and think about their own family. Prompt them with questions such as, "How is your family alike or different from this tribe?" Additionally, you can discuss ways these tribes are the same and different from one another. As they look at these different tribes around the world, marking them on the maps shows them that tribes truly can be found in different areas. Understanding yourself in the greater context of the world can be hard for your student; this activity roots them in this idea.

Practice (Indigenous People from your Area)
Provide support to your student as they research online the lives of an Indigenous group in their area. Make sure as your student does their research that they consult credible sources. Credible online sources will be unbiased and backed with evidence. The best resource is often the official tribe website. In this activity, your student will locate their tribe on a country map; you will need to provide them with this map. A map for your country can be found using a quick online search. Your student may need guidance in locating their tribe. As they research, have your student focus on what they are interested in learning about the tribe whether it be their art, stories, or history. Offer support to your student as needed.

Learning Styles

Auditory learners may enjoy recording themselves listing the facts they learn about the local Indigenous tribe or nation through their research project.

Visual learners may enjoy creating simple illustrations for each shelter or home they learn about.

Kinesthetic learners may enjoy visiting a local park to look for natural resources that Indigenous tribes or nations could use.

LESSON 53
Indigenous People in Your Area

Extension Activities

Creating a Map
Ask your student to create a large map of their country. They will add an illustration of the home for the tribe or Indigenous nation they researched in the correct spot on the map. Have them also illustrate some of the natural resources that can be found in the area.

Books
Take your student to the library or bookstore to find books written by Indigenous people. Some suggestions; *We Are Water Protectors* by Carole Lindstrom, *Fry Bread: A Native American Family Story* by Kevin Noble Maillard, *Hiawatha and the Peacemaker* by Robbie Robertson, *Jingle Dancer* by Cynthia Leitich Smith, and *Kamik: An Inuit Puppy Story* by Donald Uluadluak. Discuss with your student the different cultures in these books and how they are similar and different from their own culture.

Answer Key

Explore
Drawings will vary, but should be based on their home or a place they stay.

Write *(What are two common names for a group of Indigenous people?)*
Tribe and Nation

Write *(What resource did Inuits use to build igloos?)*
Ice

Practice *(Indigenous People Near You)*
Answers will vary. Guide and support your student as they discover their local tribe on the map provided and answer the questions as they research.

Sidebar *(Online Connection)*
Both the female and male structure types are used for homes. Both used any type of wood that could be found locally. The male hogans are more rounded than the female hogans and the male hogans are used for ceremonial purposes. Female hogans have six to eight sides and are used more for modern homes of the Navajo.

Show What You Know
1. C
2. D
3. B
4. A
5. C
6. A
7. Answers will vary. Possible answers: where the nation or tribe is located, the name of the tribe or nation, and two things about their culture

LESSON 54
Indigenous Natural Resources

Lesson Objectives

By the end of this lesson, your student will be able to:

- identify the natural resources used by Indigenous people in your region or area
- describe how Indigenous people used the resources around them
- explain common attitudes of Indigenous people toward those resources

Supporting Your Student

Explore
Before categorizing the resources, ask your student to explain the difference between a human-made resource and a natural resource. If they are confused, give more examples of each and write them on a T-chart (one side human-made and the other natural). For example, fish are a natural resource, and cups are a human-made resource. It would also be helpful for your student to come up with their own examples.

Read (Natural Resources in Your Area)
After reading this section, help your student research an Indigenous group in their area or region. In the search engine, type "Indigenous nations near [your region]." Next search, "[Indigenous nation in your area] natural resources." If you have trouble finding information, you can also search "[Indigenous nation in your area] homes made from" or "[Indigenous nation in your area] food." It would be helpful to create a two-column list with one side for the natural resources and the other side for how they are used. This will also help answer the writing section.

Practice
Before drawing how your student honors Earth, have them create a list of ways they honor Earth and ways they would like to honor Earth. Some examples are recycling, local park cleanup, reusing materials, using less, and being in nature. This will help give your student ideas to draw. Encourage them to use many details in their drawing, like a background and multiple elements.

Learning Styles

Auditory learners may enjoy hearing Indigenous people's songs using different drums, like the water drum.

Visual learners may enjoy viewing a variety of images of natural resources or seeing the items in person.

Kinesthetic learners may enjoy going on a hunt for natural resources in their local community. They may also enjoy community work in preservation.

Extension Activities

Create Your Own Drum
For this you will need an empty carton or jar, a balloon with the bottom half cut off, a rubber band, stickers, markers, and two unsharpened pencils. Have your student place the cut balloon over the carton or jar opening. Once the top of the balloon is taut, place the rubber band around it to secure the balloon. Next, have your student decorate the drum. Then use the unsharpened pencils as drumsticks.

Nature Walk
Go on a hike or walk. Look around for natural resources and think about how they might be used by people.

Answer Key

LESSON 54
Indigenous Natural Resources

natural

natural

human-made

natural

human-made

human-made

1. True
2. A
3. C
4. B
5. A
6. Possible answers: The natural resources in this picture are moose, water, trees, rocks, and plants. Moose can be used for food, clothing, and shelter. The trees can be used for shelter or making tools to hunt. The water is used for bathing and drinking. Some of the plants could be used for food or medicine.
7. Answers will vary.

Write *(What is one way Indigenous people used their natural resources?)*
Answers will vary. Possible answers: The Iroquois tribe in northeast America created a drum from animal skins and wood. The Zulu of Africa ate the land's natural resources of vegetables and grains. The bowls and spoons they used were made from wood. In Thailand, the women of the Akha Hill Tribe use the natural resources cotton, silver, shells, and bird feathers to create beautiful headdresses.

Write *(What natural resources were available to the Indigenous people of your area for food, water, and shelter?)*
Answers will vary based on your student's area.

Practice
Pictures will vary. Possible drawings may include recycling, planting a tree, or enjoying nature. The picture should have a background.

Show What You Know

LESSON 55
Indigenous People's Food

Lesson Objectives

By the end of this lesson, your student will be able to:

- describe the types of foods eaten by the Indigenous people of different regions
- identify ways Indigenous people get the foods they eat

Supporting Your Student

Explore
Before reading it would be helpful to review natural resources and human-made resources. In the "Indigenous Natural Resources" lesson, review the Explore section with your student. When answering the questions, it would be helpful to explore their kitchen or garden to help your student come up with ideas of natural foods in their house.

Read (Hunting and Fishing, Agriculture, Gathering)
These sections are examples of how Indigenous people got their food. It would be helpful to write these details down on a graphic organizer as you read. For example, you could write down each method under a heading titled "Ways Indigenous People Got Their Food." Have your student draw or write an example of hunting, fishing, agriculture (farming), and gathering.

Practice
To search for natural food in your area in the search engine, type "[area] natural foods." To help your student discover how the food was used by Indigenous people, search "[Indigenous nation] dishes or diets." It would also be helpful to create a list of the foods found in your area and see which ones the Indigenous grew or hunted. Ask your student if the foods they grew and hunted are similar to or different from the foods we find now?

Learning Styles

Auditory learners may enjoy creating a podcast explaining the different ways Indigenous people got their food.

Visual learners may enjoy watching videos about various tribes' hunting and farming practices.

Kinesthetic learners may enjoy a game of charades reviewing the new vocabulary words. They may also enjoy trying foods Indigenous people of their area enjoyed.

Extension Activities

Corn Craft
One of the main food groups for most Indigenous people in North America is corn, also called maize. This corn is found in colorful varieties. Have your student cut a basic ear of corn shape out of white cardstock. Your student will then use pencil erasers to stamp brown, orange, and yellow paint to look like corn kernels inside their ear of corn.

Traditional Food
Have your student research an Indigenous group from another area. Have your student identify the food sources of the Indigenous people and how they may vary from those found in their own area.

Answer Key

LESSON 55
Indigenous People's Food

Explore
Answers will vary. Possible answers: Ice cream is my favorite food, and I need to go to the store to get it. Apples are my favorite food and can be grown in my backyard.

(Lists of foods will vary based on items found in individual kitchens.)

Write *(What did nomadic Indigineous people eat?)*
Answer: They usually hunted big animals that traveled in herds.

Write *(What was a common way that settled Indigenous people got their food?)*
Answer: They practiced farming.

Practice
Answers will vary based on the Indigneous people's area.

Show What You Know
1. B
2. C
3. A
4. True
5. True
6. True
7. Possible answers: Indigenous people get their food by fishing, hunting, farming, and gathering food.

LESSON 56
Culture of Indigenous People

Lesson Objectives

By the end of this lesson, your student will be able to:
- explain how different Indigenous groups have different cultures
- analyze things that have changed the culture and ways of life of Indigenous people in different regions

Supporting Your Student

Read *(Indigenous People)*
You may want to discuss the differences between the words *Indigenous* and *ancestors*. *Indigenous* refers to the first group of people in an area. *Ancestors* is a word that refers to a person's relatives from a long time ago. All people have ancestors, but not all people are related to Indigenous people. Their ancestors may have moved to their region after the region began.

Write *(Who are Indigenous people? Could descendants of the Indigenous people still be living in an area?)*
Direct your student to the definition of Indigenous to answer the first question. For the second question, you may want to use a general family tree. Pretend that the oldest members are Indigenous people because they first lived in the region before anyone else. Then move further down the tree to show the youngest people. Explain how they are related to the Indigenous people and how old the youngest people are. This can show that it is possible for descendants of Indigenous people to still be alive today.

Practice
These three groups of Indigenous people are described in the reading sections. Your student may want to reread about these three groups and take notes so they know what to write in this activity.

Learning Styles

Auditory learners may enjoy listening to documentaries or podcasts about modern Indigenous groups living in their region.

Visual learners may enjoy making a collage of an Indigenous people group out of pictures printed from the internet.

Kinesthetic learners may enjoy making traditional Indigenous recipes from two or three different Indigenous groups.

Extension Activities

Read About Another
Encourage your student to explore and research a lesser-known Indigenous group. Then have your student explain what they have learned about this group.

Matching
Find pictures of different Indigenous groups around the world. You may choose the same groups from the worktext so that your student is familiar with them. Print each picture and show it to your student. See if your student can match the picture to the Indigenous group.

LESSON 56
Culture of Indigenous People

Answer Key

Write *(Who are Indigenous people? Could descendants of the Indigenous people still be living in an area?)*
Answers will vary. Possible answers: Indigenous people are the first group of people who lived in a particular place. Descendants of the Indigenous people could still live in that area today.

Practice
Answers will vary. Possible answers: Mayans live in Mexico, speak Spanish, and make crafts. Inuits speak Cree and other languages, and have hobbies like storytelling, dancing, and playing music. Hmong live in southeast Asia, herd animals, and grow rice.

Show What You Know
1. Indigenous people
2. Culture
3. Ancestors
4. Mayans
5. Canada
6. dance
7. Hmong

LESSON 57
Art of Indigenous People

Lesson Objectives

By the end of this lesson, your student will be able to:
- identify different types of art Indigenous people created
- analyze the way Indigenous people used art to record important ideas and events

Supporting Your Student

Explore
As your student looks at artwork online and in books, ask what they notice about the different kinds of artwork, what messages they think it communicates, and what the artwork tells them about Indigenous people's way of life. Help your student navigate the virtual tour of the American Indian museum. Stop the virtual tour a few times to ask questions about the artwork they see, the ways of life they notice, and any other features of American Indian life that they find interesting.

Read (Art of Indigenous People)
When reading, encourage your student to make connections to what they have learned about the art of Indigenous people. You can ask them things like "Why do they use symbols in their art? How do you think their art can teach survival? How does their art symbolize their way of life?" Have your student reread the text before writing answers to questions. Have them say answers out loud to you before writing.

Practice (Artwork)
When your student is drawing pictures of artwork that highlights your background and culture, give suggestions on what you think should be included or remind them of specific traditions your family shares.

Read (Ceramics and Pottery)
When reading this section, ask your student if they have ever seen a kiln. Look up some pictures of kilns and people using them to create pottery. Brainstorm about what this reminds you of that you do at home. Have your student reread the text before answering questions. They can say it out loud before writing in their own words.

Practice (Art Sorting)
Review with your student the different types of Indigenous art mentioned. Together find more examples of this art online. You can print some of these examples out and have your student put them into sorting categories by type of artwork. Ask, "How do you know this piece of art belongs in this group?" If your student is having difficulty, you can research specific forms of art and what they look like and do the activity again.

Learning Styles

Auditory learners may enjoy doing an oral report using pictures they found of different types of art, explaining each one.

Visual learners may enjoy using markers or watercolors to create their own kind of storytelling through art.

Kinesthetic learners may enjoy acting out how an Indigenous person would create a piece of art. For example, they could pretend to be making a sculpture out of random materials.

Extension Activities

Reading Together
Read or find a read aloud video for *Fry Bread: A Native American Family Story* by Kevin Noble Maillard. It is the story of an Indigenous recipe handed down through generations by a family as a way to keep their culture strong. Have your student discuss a similar recipe handed down in their family. Have them draw a picture of this meal with details identifying foods used to make it and any significance it has to their culture.

Answer Key

Write *(Name two things that Indigenous art*

LESSON 57
Art of Indigenous People

represents. What is Indigenous art based on?)
Indigenous art represents symbols to describe stories and it also teaches survival and how to use their land. It is based on tradition and cultures in their region.

Write *(What do Indigenous people create pottery from? Where do they heat the clay to make the pottery? Can you think of a time you (and an adult) created something in an oven?)*
They created pottery from crushed rocks and plant and animal life stuck at the bottom of rivers. They heat the clay in a kiln. Possible answers: baking a cake or creating a Christmas ornament.

Show What You Know
1. True
2. traditions, culture
3. Answers will vary. Possible answers include carvings, sculptures, pottery, weaving, and string art.

LESSON 58
Folklore From the Indigenous People

Lesson Objectives

By the end of this lesson, your student will be able to:

- describe folklore from the Indigenous people in your region or area
- recognize that folklore from Indigenous people often has a lesson or message to learn

Supporting Your Student

Online Connection
With your student, watch a video of the story of Onatah, stopping along the way to summarize what is happening and questioning why this story was written to explain something in nature. Ask guiding questions, like "What about nature are they emphasizing?," "What do you think important harvests were for the Native Americans?," and "What do you think we have learned about learning to farm from the Native Americans?" Explore online pictures of Native American harvests.

Read *(What Is Folklore?)*
Have your student read this section and explain to you what they believe that folklore is. If necessary, have them reread or discuss parts they may find confusing.

Read *(How Folklore Is Spread)*
Discuss some common folktales with your student. Refer back to any you have read together and research others together. Discuss characters they remember and whether they recognize the moral lessons taught by the stories.

Learning Styles

Auditory learners may enjoy listening to or reading folktales aloud.

Visual learners may enjoy creating a poster for a folktale that teaches a lesson.

Kinesthetic learners may enjoy singing and dancing to songs of Indigenous people that teach values or traditions.

Extension Activities

Three Sisters Garden
Have your student plant or draw a Three Sisters trio garden. Look at the garden daily and have your student observe and describe what they see, or have them draw pictures of what the plants look like growing. Have your student observe what the plants look like helping each other.

Researching Recipes
Have your student research recipes for the vegetables found in the Three Sisters trio. Have them find one that sounds good and make it together. Have your student look up the nutritional value of these foods. Discuss why these foods were important to the Native Americans to keep their families fed and healthy.

LESSON 58
Folklore From the Indigenous People

Answer Key

Write *(What is the purpose of a folktale? Can you think of a folktale that taught you a lesson?)*
Answers will vary. Possible answer: Folktales teach lessons and values. One example is "The Tortoise and the Hare," which teaches you not to be overconfident and instead keep working steadily.

Practice
1. folktale
2. jewelry
3. totem pole

Show What You Know
4. True
5. False
6. True
7. folklore
8. legend
9. nature

LESSON 59
Artifacts of Indigenous People

Lesson Objectives

By the end of this lesson, your student will be able to:
- identify types of artifacts of the Indigenous people
- identify an example of an artifact of the Indigenous people in your region or area

Supporting Your Student

Online Connection
When looking at pictures of artifacts online, discuss what is similar to and different from the ones you found. Point out some artifacts that seem to come from the same group of people.

When watching the video, pause every few minutes to discuss what the archeologists are doing. Remind your student what role archeologists and historians play in defining our past and learning about our ancestors. Ask your student, "Did you ever find something in the soil or on the street that made you curious where it came from?"

Find a local museum that has a virtual tour and look at the displays you see. Do you recognize any artifacts of the community highlighted? What are the artifacts telling us about this Indigenous community?

Read *(What Are Artifacts?)*
Discuss the different types of artifacts with your student and refer back to those you found online at the beginning of the lesson. It might be helpful after reading to point to the pictures you found and have your student repeat what type of artifact it is. While your student is reading this section, ask if they know of an artifact they have in their home that represents their cultures or traditions. Tell them to explain it to you. Ask your student, "What kind of stories can an artifact tell you?"

Learning Styles

Auditory learners may enjoy listening to an Indigenous story online about artifacts that are important to them.

Visual learners may enjoy looking at artifacts online and drawing some of their favorites.

Kinesthetic learners may enjoy acting out stories an artifact may tell about the Indigenous people who created it.

Extension Activities

Take a Virtual Museum Tour
With your student, visit a museum online from your community or a different community that displays artifacts of Indigenous people.

Researching Artifacts
Help your student find pictures of artifacts online. Have your student answer the following questions:

1. What do you believe is the purpose of this artifact?
2. What type of person used this artifact?
3. What does this artifact tell you about the culture of the civilization it came from?
4. What region of the world does this artifact come from?

Answer Key

LESSON 59
Artifacts of Indigenous People

Write *(Name three examples of artifacts.)*
Answers will vary. Possible answers: pottery, stone tools, weapons, decorative artwork, bones

Practice
Answers will vary.

Write *(You have learned that artifacts can tell us about the Indigenous group that created it. Describe some artifacts of Native American tribes that have added to our understanding of these groups.)*
Have your student think about what these items represented in these Indigenous groups. Answers will vary. Possible answers: The Navajo had wool blankets, dreamcatchers, and even bows and arrows to represent their group. The Aztecs were known for a carved stone calendar that showed their gods. The Iroquois created pots with round bottoms made of clay.

Show What You Know
This artifact is made of <u>metal</u>. The color of this artifact is <u>silver</u>. This artifact is a <u>mask</u>.

LESSON 60
Indigenous People Around the World

Lesson Objectives

By the end of this lesson, your student will be able to:
- describe the Indigenous people who lived in a region or country different from your own
- locate where Indigenous people lived on a map
- describe the shelters and housing built by Indigenous people

Supporting Your Student

Explore
Support your student by helping them do research online. Help them look up the climate and landscape of the region they choose, and guide them as they search for images and information about the shelters Indigenous people in this region typically built. When discussing the types of shelter built in this region, make sure your student is connecting to why the people of that region built shelters the way they did. Did it protect from certain kinds of weather? Was it made using resources that were abundant in the region?

Read *(Indigenous People)*
Activate your student's prior knowledge by asking them what they know (or think they know) about Indigenous people. Do any tribal nations have lands or cultural centers near where you live? Has your student ever had any experiences with Indigenous people or history?

After your student reads this section, look up pictures of First Nations and Inuit groups. Ask, "What is similar about the two groups? What is different about the two groups? What do you think their region of Canada is like?" At this point you may encourage your student to do some research on areas in Canada if they want to focus on one of these groups.

Read *(Types of Shelter)*
On a separate sheet of paper, have your student make quick sketches of the different types of shelters they have observed through this lesson. Ask them about what the shelters have in common and what makes them different.

Learning Styles

Auditory learners may enjoy listening to an Indigenous person talk about their community and culture.

Visual learners may enjoy seeing photos of different Indigenous communities in Canada as well as Indigenous communities within the region you live.

Kinesthetic learners may enjoy building a house with popsicle sticks and showing all the different parts of the house while building.

Extension Activities

Research
Look up information about the Aboriginal people of Australia. Learn about their culture, language, dress, shelter, and customs. Ask, "How are they different from the Indigenous people you have already learned about?"

Visit a Cultural Center
If your student lives near a tribal cultural center, plan a visit to learn more about the Indigenous people nearby. If there isn't one, search for virtual field trip videos online of the nearest Indigeouns tribal nation to get a first-hand view of this nation's culture and history.

LESSON 60
Indigenous People Around the World

Answer Key

Write *(If you were to live in one of these houses, which would you pick? Why?)*
Answers will vary. Possible answers: If I could choose one of these shelters to live in, I would pick a longhouse. I would pick a longhouse because it seems like it would have plenty of room for me and my family and be more comfortable.

Show What You Know
1. B
2. C
3. A
4. True
5. True
6. First Nations, Inuit, or Métis

LESSON 61
Natural Resources Used by Indigenous People

Lesson Objectives

By the end of this lesson, your student will be able to:

- identify the natural resources used by Indigenous people who lived in a region or country different from their own

Supporting Your Student

Read *(Natural Resources)*
Help your student to fully understand the connection between natural resources and survival for Indigenous people. Pause during the reading to ask questions and provide explanations. Asking questions like the following can help provide clarity:

- What kinds of natural resources did they use?
- What did they make from those natural resources?
- Why were those things important to them?

Write *(Why do the Indigenous Australians value natural resources?)*
Your student is learning how Indigenous people used the natural resources in their region to survive. Indigenous people survived by using natural resources to make tools, shelter, medicine, and food. Your student should be able to compare and contrast how Indigenous people survived and how we survive today. Your student may benefit from you modeling how to think about these differences and similarities. For example, today we use bait and nets to catch fish, while Indigenous people use spears. Today most of us go to grocery stores to purchase food, while Indigenous people hunt and gather their food.

Learning Styles

Auditory learners may enjoy watching documentaries that highlight ways Indigenous people used natural resources to survive.

Visual learners may enjoy drawing a picture with a label that explains how Indigenous people used several different resources in their region to survive.

Kinesthetic learners may enjoy taking one of the natural resources and using it like an Indigenous child would to play a game.

Extension Activities

Research and Make
The didgeridoo is a wind instrument developed by the Indigenous Aboriginal people of Australia. The Indigenous people used natural resources to make this instrument. Research how to make your own didgeridoo with resources you have on hand in your home or environment.

Using Resources
Take your student out for a walk and encourage them to make note of all the natural resources around their neighborhood. Then, ask your student how they could use these natural resources to create a shelter, tools, and other necessities. If possible, have your student create a tool out of natural resources they found on their walk.

Answer Key

Explore

LESSON 61
Natural Resources Used by Indigenous People

Answers will vary. Possible answers: All the images are of natural resources. The shelter and boomerang were made from natural resources, and the fruit in the picture is a natural resource too.

Write *(Why do the Indigenous Australians value natural resources?)*
Answers will vary. Possible answer: They value natural resources because they use them to survive.

Write *(How are the homes pictured here alike? How are the homes different?)*
Answers will vary. Possible answers: They have similar roofs. Their walls are also both made of sticks and branches. They are different shapes and are from different parts of the world. Indigenous people used natural resources from their environment. These resources provided only basic shelter, which was sufficient for their survival.

Write *(Why were tools and weapons important to Indigenous Australians?)*
Answers will vary. Possible answer: Indigenous people used tools as weapons for protection. They also used tools for hunting and gathering food.

Practice
Answers will vary based on where your student lives.

Show What You Know
1. B
2. B
3. False

LESSON 62
What Indigenous People Ate

Lesson Objectives

By the end of this lesson, your student will be able to:

- describe the types of foods eaten by Indigenous people who lived in a region or country different from their own and how they got those foods

Supporting Your Student

Write *(How would hunting and gathering be different on a prairie than in the rain forest?)*
Assist your student in generating their response by asking the following guiding questions: "Would the tribe in the desert be able to catch fish? Would the tribe near the ocean be able to hunt for buffalo?" Guide your student to the chart in the Read "Indigenous Diets in Different Regions" section and have them identify what foods would be in the prairie and the rain forest.

Read *(Indigenous Meals)*
It may be helpful to pull up some photographs of Indigenous foods while your student is reading this section so they can get a better idea of how Indigenous foods were similar to and different from the foods we eat today. Another idea is to show them a video of how popcorn was made over an open fire and have your student describe how making popcorn was different back then compared to the microwave popcorn we eat today.

Practice
You can support your student by helping them label the food they draw for their indigenous feast. If they are not sure what to draw, refer back to the Read "Indigenous Diets of Different Regions" section to find some options of foods that they could add to their meal. Remind them to make sure all the foods they choose would be found in their particular region.

Learning Styles

Auditory learners may enjoy listening to traditional Indigenous music while they are working.

Visual learners may enjoy watching videos about Indigenous foods from all around the world.

Kinesthetic learners may enjoy making an indigenous meal out of modeling clay or cooking a real indigenous food such as popcorn or corn bread in the kitchen!

Extension Activities

Foraging Walk
With your student, go to a local park or a place outside with some plants and animals. Encourage your student to pretend that they are hunters and gatherers. Ask your student what they could find to eat if they were members of an Indigenous tribe living on this land.

Make a Bow and Arrow
Help your student create a bow and arrow using a curved stick and a string. Supervise your student while they practice shooting the bow and arrow at a safe target, such as a tower of plastic cups. After using their makeshift bow, ask your student if they think it would be easier to be a hunter or a gatherer.

Answer Key

In the Real World

LESSON 62
What Indigenous People Ate

Answers will vary. You might use a search engine to find out if any of the plants or animals that you see are edible.

Explore
Answers will vary. Possible answers: sandwiches, tacos, spaghetti, pizza

Take a Closer Look
Answers will vary. If your student did not include any foods that are special to their culture, you might help them research what some of those foods are.

Write *(How would hunting and gathering be different on a prairie than in the rain forest?)*
Answers will vary. Possible answers: On the prairie, the tribe could not catch fish. They would hunt for bison and rabbits. In the rain forest, they would eat fish and alligators. Tribes from both Indigenous regions could grow corn and other crops.

Practice
Answers will vary. Possible answers: If choosing an Indigenous tribe from the Arctic, your student may draw fish, shellfish, berries, and potatoes. If choosing a tribe from the woodlands, your student may draw a squirrel, corn, beans, pumpkin, and berries.

Show What You Know
1. gatherers
2. ice
3. corn
4. medicine
5. hunters
6. potatoes
7. rain forest
8. fire
9. Answers will vary. Possible answers: The Indigenous people found plants and animals near their homes to eat. There were different plants and animals in the different regions where Indigenous people lived.

LESSON 63
How Indigenous People Live

Lesson Objectives

By the end of this lesson, your student will be able to:

- describe the culture and the ways of life of the Indigenous people who lived in a region or country different from their own

Supporting Your Student

Explore
For this section, you can help your student by filling in the chart about your family's culture. Discuss elements of your family's culture such as food you eat, clothing you wear for special occasions, holidays you celebrate, and any other family traditions. Discuss what makes your family unique from other families.

Read *(Music)*
As your student reads this section of text, help them pronounce the Indigenous musical instruments.

- didgeridoo: DI·jr·ee·doo
- djembe: JEM·bay
- mbira: em·BEE·ruh

Write *(What do you wear on special occasions? How is it similar and different to the regalia of Indigenous tribes?)*
Assist your student in generating their responses to these questions by prompting them to look at the photographs in the "Clothing" section of text. Ask the following guiding questions: "What do you wear when you get dressed up for a special event (such as attending a wedding or church)? How is that similar and different to the clothing in the photographs?" Help them compare their own clothing to that worn by the Indigenous tribes.

Online Connection
Assist your student in searching for videos of traditional Indigenous dancing. Search the keywords *Aboriginal dance*, *powwow Native American dance*, and *Zaouli African dance* to see videos of tribes from different regions.

Learning Styles

Auditory learners may enjoy listening to authentic Indigenous music while they are working.

Visual learners may enjoy looking through a family photo album to identify different examples of their family's culture.

Kinesthetic learners may enjoy taking a movement break and making their own Indigenous song or dance. You could tap out a beat and sing along while your student makes up a dance to the rhythm!

Extension Activities

Learn a Powwow Dance
There are many tutorials online teaching children the movements to powwow dances. This would be a fun activity for the whole family! Search for the keywords *powwow dance for kids* and clear some space for your student to practice their dance moves.

Indigenous Coloring Page
Print a page similar to the one below for your student to color.

LESSON 63
How Indigenous People Live

Answer Key

Explore
Answers will vary. Possible answers: My family speaks English. We like to eat hamburgers and hot dogs. We listen to R&B music.

Write *(What do you wear on special occasions? How is it similar and different to the regalia of Indigenous tribes?)*
Answers will vary. Possible answer: On special occasions, I wear pants, a button-up shirt, and a tie. This is similar because we both have special clothes. It is different because my clothes do not have beads or feathers.

Practice *(Fill In the Blanks)*
Answers will vary. Possible answer: I would wear traditional regalia. I would eat a feast. I would listen to a didgeridoo. We would dance and sing.

Show What You Know
1. True
2. False
3. True
4. False
5. True
6. False
7. True
8. True

LESSON 64
Comparing Culture to That of Indigenous People

Lesson Objectives

By the end of this lesson, your student will be able to:

- describe the art and ways of life of the Indigenous people who lived in a region or country different from their own

Supporting Your Student

Explore
In this section, you can support your student by helping them identify art throughout their home. Remember, art is more than just the frames hanging on the walls! Look for unique examples of art and culture, such as pottery (purchased or handmade), poems, movies, family photographs, or pictures that your student drew. Assist your student in locating at least three examples of art within their home.

Read *(Physical Indigenous Art)*
You can assist your student in this section by helping them to understand the difference between physical and conceptual art. This can be a tricky thing for second graders to comprehend. It may be helpful to explain some other things that are conceptual (e.g., dreams, language, games) and compare them to physical things to help your student understand the difference.

Write *(Why did Indigenous people sing and dance?)*
Assist your student in responding to this question by asking the following guiding questions: "When did Indignous people typically sing and dance? What were some of the reasons they might be celebrating or gathering?" Guide your student to the Read "Conceptional Indigenous Arts" section or the lesson titled "Culture of Indigenous People" to review why Indigenous people sing and dance.

Learning Styles

Auditory learners may enjoy listening to traditional Indigenous music while they work.

Visual learners may enjoy searching online for more examples of Indigenous artwork.

Kinesthetic learners may enjoy taking a brain break to create an art project of their choosing.

Extension Activities

Totem Pole
Have your student build a totem pole out of toilet paper tubes. Give them one tube for each member in their family, and have them represent each family member with a different animal. For ideas on different animals to design, show them a few photographs of different totem poles online before they begin.

Paper Weaving
Cut two different colors of construction paper into long strips that are one inch wide. Have your student lay one color of strips down on the table with a small space between each strip. With the second color, weave the strips over/under the first color until all strips are used and your child has created a woven paper textile of their own.

LESSON 64
Comparing Culture to That of Indigenous People

Answer Key

Explore
Answers will vary. Possible answers: pictures of family photographs, a decorative vase, any artwork hanging on the wall

Write *(Which one is your favorite?)*
Answers will vary. Possible answer: My favorite art in our home is a photograph of our family. I like this art because I love my family, and it reminds me how much I love them when I see it.

Write *(Why did Indigenous people sing and dance?)*
Answers will vary. Possible answer: Indigenous people would sing and dance to celebrate special occasions, celebrate life and death, and tell stories.

Show What You Know
1. C
2. A
3. E
4. B
5. D
6. physical art
7. physical art
8. conceptual art
9. conceptual art

LESSON 65
Folklore of Indigenous People

Lesson Objectives

By the end of this lesson, your student will be able to:

- describe the folklore and ways of life of the Indigenous people who lived in a region or country different from your own and identify the message

Supporting Your Student

In the Real World

Monitor and guide your student's search for emotional commercials. You can offer suggestions if you have examples in mind. Ask your student guiding questions: How does this commercial make you feel? What does the story do to bring up those feelings for you? Do you think other people feel the same way? Do you think this makes people feel connected, knowing they share similar feelings?

Explore

If your student is having a hard time thinking of stories that are told in their family, help to jog their memory by asking about their relatives. You might ask: What did your (grandma, grandpa, aunt, etc.) do for a living? Did (your family member) have siblings? Do they ever talk about their (work/sibling/parents/pets)? From there, try to tease out stories they may have been told.

Write *(What is your favorite fairy tale? What important message or lesson do you think it tells?)*

Review some popular fairy tales with your student and allow them to choose one that is their favorite. Discuss what some of the lessons are from that fairy tale.

Learning Styles

Auditory learners may enjoy retelling aloud a story they have heard from a grandparent that represents a family custom or belief.

Visual learners may enjoy making drawings of their favorite family gathering or shared celebration.

Kinesthetic learners may enjoy teaching a friend a dance that is done during family gatherings.

Extension Activities

Read a Folktale
Read *Johnny Appleseed* by Steven Kellogg. You can also find a read-aloud video version online.

1. Do a shared reading of *Johnny Appleseed*.
2. After the book is read, go to the front page that talks about what a folktale is.
3. Talk to your student about this definition.
4. Ask: What is your favorite part of this folktale?
5. Have your student write their answer, and then discuss.

Storytelling Competition
Have your student watch videos online of storytelling competition winners. Search for "children's storytelling competition" or "storytelling competition" to find videos (though you may want to preview the selections before viewing with your student). Ask your student what they observe about storytelling and how to do it well. Have your student practice telling a favorite fairy tale or folktale before performing it for you (and/or their family).

LESSON 65
Folklore of Indigenous People

Answer Key

Write *(What is your favorite fairy tale? What important message or lesson do you think it tells?)*

Answers will vary. Possible answer: Cinderella is my favorite fairy tale, and I think the lesson is that if you work hard and are kind and honest, good things will happen for you eventually.

Show What You Know
6. D
7. B
8. True

LESSON 66
Comparing Artifacts to Those of Indigenous People

Lesson Objectives

By the end of this lesson, your student will be able to:

- identify artifacts of a tribe of Indigenous people who lived in a region or country different from their own

Supporting Your Student

Online Connection
Help your student search the internet to learn about some of the most famous artifacts. There are some great resources for kids, including videos. On a video platform such as YouTube, try searching for keywords such as *"King Tut for kids."* Make sure to preview content to ensure it is age appropriate before watching with your student.

Explore
In this section, your student may be interested to learn more about what archeologists do. Spend a little time discussing the job of an archeologist as they read through this section.

Read
As your student reads all three Read sections, it may be helpful to give them a highlighter so they can highlight important information about Indigenous artifacts from each region. Assist them to compare and contrast similarities (such as hunting tools) and differences (such as cultural items).

Learning Styles

Auditory learners may enjoy listening to an archeologist talk about their job and some of the interesting artifacts they have discovered.

Visual learners may enjoy searching for other famous artifacts from other cultures and time periods as well.

Kinesthetic learners may enjoy visiting a museum to see more examples of artifacts from around the world.

Extension Activities

Jell-O Dig
Create a fun archeological dig without leaving your kitchen! Use a large plastic container or baking dish. Add some "treasures" to the dish. Make sure these treasures can get wet! Some theme ideas for Jell-O and treasures include underwater (seashells, pom poms, plastic fish, blue Jell-O), ABC (letter magnets, rainbow beads, yellow Jell-O), or dinosaurs (plastic dinosaurs, bugs, green and brown beads, green Jell-O). Then using the directions on the Jell-O box, pour the Jell-O into the dish so that it covers the treasures. Put the dish in the refrigerator for three hours or until the Jell-O has congealed. Give your student an old toothbrush, chopsticks, popsicle sticks, or other small "tool" to search for the buried treasure. Let the digging begin!

Artifacts Among Us
Look around your home for examples of artifacts from older generations. Maybe you have a photo album with pictures of great-grandparents or old birthday cards from loved ones. Explain to your student how these are artifacts from your family. Encourage them to make the connection between artifacts in their life and the artifacts in the lesson.

LESSON 66
Comparing Artifacts to Those of Indigenous People

Answer Key

Write *(Pretend you are an archeologist at a Native American archeological dig site. You are sifting through the soil, when all of a sudden you spot this. What do you think this is? How would you know that this is an artifact and not just a regular rock?)*
Answers will vary. Possible answer: This is a tool or weapon. I know it is an artifact because it has a human-made appearance and it looks like it was chiseled. A natural stone would not have that texture.

Write *(Compare and contrast the Indigenous artifacts found in two different regions.)*
Answers will vary. Possible answer: Indigenous people of Australia and Africa both had weapons and tools. Australian tribes had boats and boomerangs. African tribes had masks and statues.

Show What You Know
1. Native American
2. Australian
3. African
4. Australian
5. Australian
6. African
7. C
8. A
9. D
10. D
11. C
12. arrowhead
13. statue
14. boomerang
15. mask

LESSON 67
Comparing and Contrasting Indigenous Peoples

Lesson Objectives

By the end of this lesson, your student will be able to:

- compare and contrast two groups of Indigenous people

Supporting Your Student

Take a Closer Look
Help your student make connections between what they've learned about Indigenous peoples' use of natural resources and adapting to their environments to ask guiding questions like, "Where do the Inuit live?," "What is the weather like there?," "What do you like to wear when it's extremely cold?," or "How do you think that affects the way Inuits dress?"

Create
With your student, explore some of these Indigenous communities online. Print some pictures to reflect their different lifestyles. Be sure to point out shelter, food, and any type of government organization you may notice. This may help your student pick a community to create their diorama.

Read *(Indigenous People of Canada)*
You can read this section together with your student to see if there are any apparent questions or misunderstandings before you have them read about specific groups in Canada. As they are reading, point out important facts and have them repeat to you if needed.

Read *(The Métis and the Inuits)*
As your student is reading the text, have them tell you which group they are reading about and what they are learning about them. Your student should reread the text to point out what they are thinking and any differences they may notice. This will help them with the Practice activity.

Practice
If necessary, have your student underline key information in paragraphs on each of these groups before putting it into the chart. Help your student complete the chart with one or two answers in each section.

Learning Styles

Auditory learners may enjoy listening to some music from these Indigenous groups in Canada.

Visual learners may enjoy drawing pictures of each group on one sheet of paper and describing their differences.

Kinesthetic learners may enjoy acting out a day in the life of an Indigenous person from each of these three groups. In their acting, they can display some differences they learned.

Extension Activities

Local Museum Exhibit or Online Virtual Museum Tour
With your student, look online for a nearby museum you can visit that has an exhibit on Indigenous people in your area. If this is not available, find a virtual tour online that you can take together. Stop to discuss the differences in this Indigenous community compared to the Indigenous peoples in Canada.

Interview Someone New
Find someone that has moved to your community from a faraway place and have your student interview them. Some questions they can ask:

- Why did you move to this community?
- What was the hardest part of your move?
- What is the same about where you live now from where you used to live?
- What is different about where you live now from where you used to live?

You can also have them write down other questions they would like to ask.

LESSON 67
Comparing and Contrasting Indigenous Peoples

Answer Key

Explore
Answers will vary. Possible answers: I have never visited Mexico, but Mexican food is my favorite! I love enchiladas. I know there are deserts and beaches in Mexico, and there are deserts and beaches where I live too. In my country most people speak English, and in Mexico people speak Spanish.

Write (Fill in the blanks based on what you learned. What are three facts that you learned about the First Nations people?)
1. First Nations
2. self-government
3. hunting and fishing

Answers will vary. Possible answers: Their culture developed around the harsh climate and respect for the land and the animals. There were more than 1.3 million people in Canada who identified as First Nations. Each First Nation had self-government. They all developed systems of government and cultures. Most First Nations of Canada lived mainly from hunting and fishing. They migrated seasonally to get food.

Practice
Answers will vary. Possible answers:

First Nations: developed around the harsh climate and respect for the land and the animals, had self-government, developed systems of government and cultures, lived mainly from hunting and fishing, migrated seasonally to get food.

Métis: began when European settlers married Indigenous women; had their own history, culture, founding stories, languages, flag, and way of life; were skilled hunters and trappers

Inuits: descended from the Thule people; wore warm boots called mukluks, lived in tents in the summer and igloos in the winter, ate meat, fish, and berries

Show What You Know
4. True
5. True
6. False
7. True
8. Answers will vary. Possible answers: includes at least one difference between the two groups and one similarity. Once they have done this, encourage them to find something else that is different to add to their short essay.

LESSON 68
Sites and Monuments of Indigenous Cultures

Lesson Objectives

By the end of this lesson, your student will be able to:

- identify and describe Indigenous cultural sites or monuments found today in their country

Supporting Your Student

Read *(Monuments Remember and Honor the Past)*
In this section, your student will learn how monuments connect us to the past and help us understand history. Also, monuments and cultural sites honor and remember those who lived here thousands of years ago. By looking at monuments, we can often look into the culture of the people they represent.

Read *(Historical Monuments in the United States)*
Before your student begins reading, ask "Do you know of any monuments that represent an important part of our history?" and "Why do you think it was an important monument?"

Before reading make sure to take a look at the pictures of each monument to see if your student knows where it is located.

Practice *(Cultural Site)*
In this section, you will be looking at a website with your student and discovering some new places in the country that show monuments and represent cultures of Native American Indigenous groups that lived here thousands of years ago. Take time to go through reading and looking at the website with your student to discover all of these significant cultural sites in America.

Learning Styles

Auditory learners may enjoy listening to an audio tour of an Indigenous monument.

Visual learners may enjoy printing pictures of famous monuments and creating a collage.

Kinesthetic learners may enjoy sculpting or building a model of an Indigenous monument.

Extension Activities

Visit a Museum
Go online to find a local museum that has a display of monuments or cultural representation of Indigenous people in your area. Visit the museum and have your student create a drawing of what they saw with explanations of each. They could request a brochure while there to help with this activity.

Washington, D.C.
If you cannot visit Washington, D.C., search online for a video about it and watch it with your student. Highlight various points of interest and history that are important. Stop the video periodically to discuss what they are learning.

LESSON 68
Sites and Monuments of Indigenous Cultures

Answer Key

Write *(Why are monuments important in American society, and how do they reflect their Indigenous groups?)*
Answers will vary. Possible answers: A monument represents and honors Indigenous people who lived in an area thousands of years ago.

Write *(Name three monuments that represent United States history.)*
Answers will vary. Possible answers: Lincoln Memorial, Washington Monument, and Statue of Liberty

Practice
Your student will need assistance choosing a cultural and historical site. Answers will vary based on their choices. Please help your student discover the purpose and meaning behind each site.

Show What You Know
1. C
2. B
3. D
4. B
5. A
6. C
7. Answers will vary. Possible answer: Indigenous peoples' monuments are special places that teach others about people or events that were important. Some monuments are the actual places that people lived long ago, and you can see their buildings and things that were special to them. This keeps their history alive so people don't forget what life was like for the Indigenous people that lived there.

LESSON 69
Chapter 7 Review

Lesson Objectives

In this lesson, your student will review the following big ideas from Chapter 7:

- Indigenous people had different types of artifacts, folklore, and art. (Lessons 59, 65, and 66)
- Indigenous people lived in different regions and had different natural resources. (Lessons 60 and 61)
- Indigenous people had different types of food, culture, and distinct ways of life. (Lesson 62)
- There are monuments and cultural sites from Indigenous people that help us understand these groups and their cultures. (Lesson 68)

Supporting Your Student

Create
Assist your student as they research their chosen group of Indigenous people by asking guiding questions like, "What are some artifacts that have been found from this culture?," "Where were those artifacts found?," and "What does the traditional dress of this culture look like?"

Practice *(Vocabulary Activity)*
Have your student describe each word to you in their own words and come up with a word that means the same thing. Ask questions like, "What would a picture of that word look like?" or "How would you draw a picture to explain this word to someone who does not know much about Indigenous people?" If necessary, your student can use a phrase instead of a word that means the same as the vocabulary word.

Practice *(Compare Two Indigenous Groups)*
Help your student decide which two groups to compare. If necessary, go over the chapters that targeted specific groups in Canada and the United States. Remind your student to make sure that they find something the same and something different about the two groups to help with their writing.

Learning Styles

Auditory learners may enjoy listening to a story online about an Indigenous group they have already learned about.

Visual learners may enjoy looking online at videos and pictures of their favorite Indigenous group.

Kinesthetic learners may enjoy creating a skit and acting out a conversation between a parent and a child from an Indigenous community.

Extension Activities

Create a Timeline
Have your student choose one Indigenous group and create a timeline depicting the group's beginning, important achievements, and where they are today.

Visit a Local Museum
Using the same group as the timeline created, have your student visit a museum (in person or online) that has a display of artifacts, cultural items, and paintings depicting this society. Ask your student what else they learned by seeing the additional artifacts and artwork.

LESSON 69
Chapter 7 Review

Answer Key

Practice *(Vocabulary Activity)*
Drawings will vary. Check your student's drawings to ensure they have an understanding of each word.

Practice *(Matching)*
1. D
2. B
3. A
4. F
5. C
6. E

Practice *(Compare Two Indigenous Groups)*
Review your student's Venn diagram. If necessary go back to previous chapters and ask your student where they got their information. Make sure there are a few answers in each section.

CHAPTER 7
Assessment

Quick Review

Refer to the statement your student circled in the Show What You Know section to self-assess their knowledge of the chapter concepts. Then to assist in determining if your student is ready to take the assessment, consider:

- Having your student ask questions about Indigenous people and researching the answers online.
- Having your student write a summary comparing and contrasting two groups of Indigenous people.

CHAPTER 7
Assessment

Chapter Assessment

Project: Timeline

You will create a timeline for one of the Indigenous groups you compared using the Venn diagram in the worktext. You will identify the growth of the Indigenous community over time and include any details about migration, natural resources, and other factors that influenced their living conditions. Then you will put these events in order on the timeline.

Project Requirements or Steps:

1. Write down five changes (or events) that have happened over time in the Indigenous group.
2. Number the events in the order from 1 (first) to 5 (last).
3. Draw a line across a piece of white paper.
4. Write the events in order below the line.
5. Write the year that each event occurred above each event.

Using your timeline, write a paragraph that describes the events of the Indigenous group and when these events took place.

CHAPTER 7
Assessment

Chapter Assessment Rubric

Use the following rubric to grade your student's assessment.

	4	3	2	1	Points
Timeline	The timeline accurately conveys the events that took place and when they occurred.	The timeline somewhat conveys the events that took place and when they occurred.	The timeline conveys some events that took place but not when they occurred.	The timeline does not convey the events that took place and when they occurred.	
Paragraph	The paragraph accurately conveys the events that took place and when they occurred.	The paragraph somewhat conveys the events that took place and when they occurred.	The paragraph conveys some events that took place but not when they occurred.	The paragraph does not convey the events that took place and when they occurred.	
Grammar and Mechanics	There are no grammar or punctuation errors.	There are one or two grammar or punctuation errors.	There are several grammar or punctuation errors.	There are a distracting number of grammar or punctuation errors.	

Total Points _____/12

Average _____

CHAPTER 7
Assessment

Alternative Assessment

Use the words from the Word Bank to complete each sentence below.

Word Bank: tribes   shelter   housing   first   hunters   natural resource
folklore   artifact   tradition   ritual

1. _____ are the traditional beliefs, customs, and stories of a community, passed through the generations by word of mouth.

2. Indigenous Native Americans are believed to be the _____ people to exist in North America.

3. Some families eat foods that are special, or a _____, in their culture.

4. Indigenous people lived in groups called _____.

5. Tribes work together as _____ and gatherers to find and grow food.

6. A _____ is something found in nature that can be used by people.

7. An _____ is a manmade object that has some kind of cultural significance.

8. _____ is the place where you live that provides you protection from the weather.

9. The different styles of _____ were influenced by where they lived, as well as the climate and seasons.

10. A _____ is a ceremony in which the actions and wording follow a prescribed form and order.

CHAPTER 7
Assessment

Alternative Assessment Answer Key

1. Folklore
2. first
3. tradition
4. tribes
5. hunters
6. natural resource
7. artifact
8. Shelter
9. housing
10. ritual

LESSON 70
Explorers

Lesson Objectives

By the end of this lesson, your student will be able to:

- identify at least three explorers and where they traveled
- describe why explorers traveled to different places in the world

Supporting Your Student

Explore

If your student does not have much experience with travel, ask them about local places they may have gone without knowing what to expect to help them connect to the idea of preparing for something unknown. If they struggle to think of responses for what each person in the pictures would need to do to prepare for their journey, ask guiding questions like "What is the weather like on a mountain?" and "What kind of shoes would someone need to climb a rocky landscape?"

Read *(Why Explorers Travel)*

Talking about ancient history can be tough for your student to conceptualize. It might help to make a simple timeline with your student to illustrate how long ago the first five centuries CE were. Mark events on the timeline from their own life, like their birthday and the present day. This will help them visualize that their lifetime has been a short amount of time compared to more than 2,000 years of history.

Online Connection

Depending on the climate where you live, your student may not have experienced extreme cold. Help them visualize how extreme the polar climates are by asking them to close their eyes and picture the Arctic. Describe for them the wind, the temperature, the snow, the ice, and the lack of shelter. You might remind them of times in their life when the weather was very, very cold, and ask what that was like for them.

Practice

Your student may review the text to locate the reasons given, but they may also enjoy doing additional research on the expeditions mentioned and consider the reasons each explorer in this lesson set out on their expedition. This can help your student feel more personally connected to the concepts in the lesson.

Learning Styles

Auditory learners may enjoy listening to a podcast about explorers.

Visual learners may enjoy making their own graphic novel of one of the expeditions referenced in the lesson.

Kinesthetic learners may enjoy going on a hike somewhere unfamiliar and journaling their observations.

Extension Activities

Create a Poster

Have your student research a different explorer and create a poster. The poster should include illustrations and facts about the explorer to show where this explorer traveled and why.

Compare and Contrast

Have your student choose two of the explorers from the lesson and compare and contrast why the explorers traveled to the places they did. Your student may use a Venn diagram or other graphic organizer to record this information.

LESSON 70
Explorers

Answer Key

Practice
Answers will vary. Possible answers: to learn about what is there, to share knowledge with the world, to find new ways to trade and people to trade with, to find gold

Write
Answers will vary. Review your student's response to ensure they have appropriately named an explorer and matching expedition and explained why they made their choice.

Show What You Know
1. C
2. B
3. D
4. A
5. Answers will vary. Possible answers: Eudoxus of Cyzicus—Africa, Ferdinand Magellan—the whole world, Leif Erikson—North America, Christopher Columbus—Caribbean, Jacques Piccard—Mariana Trench, Don Walsh—Mariana Trench, Neil Armstrong—the moon, Buzz Aldrin—the moon

LESSON 71
An Explorer's Journey

Lesson Objectives

By the end of this lesson, your student will be able to:
- trace the routes of explorers on a map
- describe challenges of an explorer's journey

Supporting Your Student

Read (An Explorer's Journey)
If your student struggles to understand the meaning of challenges, they may benefit from discussing real-life problems they may face while traveling to different places. Possible questions to ask are, "What if we get lost while traveling on a vacation?," "What if there is a bad storm while we are traveling?," and "How could we solve these problems and still make it to where we are going?"

Write (List two challenges that an explorer may have faced long ago.)
It could be useful to help your student appreciate the challenges that these explorers and sailors faced by helping them understand just how bad the conditions on a ship could be. This could be done by giving them some relatable scenarios. For example, the tools that these explorers and sailors used often broke easily, so you might ask your student, "If you were trying to do your homework and the lead on your pencil kept breaking, why would that make it more challenging to do your homework?" Since the sailors slept wherever they could and the ship was often wet inside, you might ask your student, "How difficult would it be to get a good night's sleep if you had to sleep on the floor on top of a wet rug?" Questions like these could help your student connect to what these explorers faced and appreciate just how challenging these journeys were.

Practice
Supervise your student as they trace their route with their finger. If they are having difficulty, ask them to notice any over-water passages in the direction they plan to travel. You might ask additional questions like, "What if you were going to journey by land?," "Which route would you take?," and "What if you needed to travel from Athens to Tbilisi, Georgia? How would you get there?"

Learning Styles

Auditory learners may enjoy doing an oral report on the many challenges an explorer may face while on their journey.

Visual learners may enjoy watching videos about the expeditions in this lesson.

Kinesthetic learners may enjoy acting out the journey and challenges of an explorer.

Extension Activities

Write a Letter
Have your student pretend they are traveling as an explorer from long ago. Have them write a letter to their family describing the challenges they and their crew are facing while on their journey.

Exploration Travel Agent
Have your student pretend they own a travel agency. Your student should encourage and plan expeditions for explorers. Have them research three places in the world they would send explorers. Have your student create a brochure that explains why they chose to send explorers to these places, the routes they chose to send them on, and some fun facts about the location.

LESSON 71
An Explorer's Journey

Answer Key

Create
Review your student's map to ensure that they drew an upside-down map of their room.

Write *(List two challenges that an explorer may have faced long ago.)*
Answers will vary. Possible answers: bad weather, difficulty charting a route, tools that were hard to use, food spoiling, illness, rodents and other pests, lack of complete and accurate maps of the world

Practice
Answers will vary. Ensure that your student drew the best route from Oslo, Norway, to Athens, Greece.

Show What You Know
1. D
2. A
3. Answers will vary. Possible answers: compass, telescope, maps, astrolabe, stars, sextant

LESSON 72
This Land Is Your Land

Lesson Objectives

By the end of this lesson, your student will be able to:
- describe what it means to claim or own land
- identify examples of things explorers brought or sent back to their countries

Supporting Your Student

Explore
It really can be a tricky concept to think about what owning something means, and what it means for something to be "mine" (yours, theirs, etc.). Work through each set of questions with your student by asking them to think aloud while they consider their answers so you can understand their thought process.

In the example with the crayons being shared between siblings, you could say, "The crayons are for your use, but they are also for your sibling's use. They are yours, but they are also theirs. You share them. Your favorite pajamas are just yours. You own them."

Read *(Claiming Land)*
To support your student in understanding the meaning of *claim* and *own*, you can model the definition. For example, you can find something you own and use this sentence stem: "I own this _____ because it is my property. I am claiming this _____ because it belongs to me."

Practice
If your student mixes up the explorers, what they found, and where they were from, return to the reading section. Ask your student to locate certain terms to help them find what to reread. For example, "Can you find the name John Cabot on this page somewhere? Point when you find it." You can have them reread the section to themselves, or you can read it aloud together.

Learning Styles

Auditory learners may enjoy explaining what it means to claim or own land out loud to a family member.

Visual learners may enjoy researching explorers who have claimed land and then making a timeline of the explorer's life.

Kinesthetic learners may enjoy role-playing to show how an explorer finds things and takes them back to their country.

Extension Activities

Trading Cards
Have your student use note cards to make trading cards with information about different early explorers. Have your student draw a picture of the explorer and research facts about explorers to add to each card. Each card should have an illustration and facts about the early explorer.

Become an Explorer
Your student can explore their backyard or a park to note what things might be valuable to bring back to their home. You might help them see the available resources (e.g., "Those trees would make good lumber for building.").

LESSON 72
This Land Is Your Land

Answer Key

Write *(Why do you think early explorers would claim land as their own even though people were already living on the land?)*
Answers will vary. Possible answer: Early explorers felt they were more powerful than the Indigenous people of the land.

Write *(Can you think of a reason explorers would want to take gold and silver back to their countries?)*
Answers will vary. Possible answers: to help the people in their country, to help pay for expensive wars, to make the country richer

Practice
1. John Cabot: Canada, England
2. Bartolomeu Dias: Brazil, Portugal
3. Francisco Coronado: Grand Canyon, Spain

Show What You Know
4. A
5. John Cabot
6. Grand Canyon
7. Portugal
8. Answers will vary. Possible answers: silver, gold, information, sweet potatoes, corn, squash, bananas, potatoes
9. Answers will vary. Possible answer: Ships carried their riches back to Spain.

LESSON 73
Owning Land

Lesson Objectives

By the end of this lesson, your student will be able to:

- compare and contrast how explorers and Indigenous people viewed owning land

Supporting Your Student

Read *(Indigenous People)*
In order to activate prior knowledge, it might be helpful for your student to scan and skim Chapter 7 before reading this lesson. Give them a moment to scan that material, then ask a question like, "Based on what you have learned about Indigenous people, how do you think they view land?" This can be an open response without a right answer. It is meant to initiate active reading.

Write *(Why do you think explorers wanted the land that they owned to be their own private property?)*
If your student has a hard time thinking of ideas for this question, have the student think about things that they own. Do they have some things that they do not like to share? If so, ask them to list the reasons why they do not like to share those items. You may use their home as an example to discuss private property.

Practice
It may be helpful to review that *compare* means similar and *contrast* means different. Use examples from your student's life to help them understand. Here is an example: "Think about spaghetti and macaroni. They are similar because they are both pasta dishes, so we could put that in the middle. But spaghetti is usually served with tomato sauce, and macaroni is usually served with cheese sauce."

Learning Styles

Auditory learners may enjoy doing an oral report on how Indigenous people viewed owning land.

Visual learners may enjoy looking at digital maps that show the changes in land claims in North America since the 1500s.

Kinesthetic learners may enjoy creating their Venn diagram in chalk on a driveway or sidewalk.

Extension Activities

Land Owner
Your student can pretend that their bedroom is land they own. On a separate piece of paper, have them list several items that are very valuable to them. They should consider why they are valuable and what it would be like to suddenly lose access to their room and resources. What if one day someone was standing guard outside their room and they could not go in or use their things anymore? Have them explain their answer.

Slide Deck
Using a computer, your student can create a slide deck with information comparing and contrasting how Indigenous people and explorers viewed owning land. Have them place information on a chart or table and add images to make their slides more appealing.

Answer Key

Write *(Why do you think explorers wanted the*

LESSON 73
Owning Land

land that they owned to be their own private property?)

Answers will vary. Possible answers: Explorers wanted the land for themselves. They wanted to claim the lands for their countries. They wanted to get rich. They wanted to control the resources.

Practice

Answers will vary. Possible answers:

Indigenous People: viewed land as a resource for all, did not believe in private ownership of land, thought of land as enjoyment and a resource for all people

Explorers: viewed land as a rich source of raw materials, natural environment was a resource that could be used for individual gain, could become very wealthy from its resources

Both: felt that they could benefit from trading resources and knowledge of land

Show What You Know

1. True
2. A
3. trading
4. Answers will vary. Possible answers: did not let people come onto the land or use the resources there without permission

LESSON 74
Explorers and Indigenous People

Lesson Objectives

By the end of this lesson, your student will be able to:

- describe ways explorers and Indigenous people interacted with each other

Supporting Your Student

Create

If your student is unfamiliar with scripts, show them some examples of scripts for children online so they can see the format. Help guide your student through the process by asking them to tell you about the situation they are thinking of before writing their script. The idea is for it to be short, so help them boil it down to the most important parts.

Write *(How do you think the Indigenous people's lives changed once the early explorers took over their land?)*

Your student may have a hard time imagining what would be different about life for the Indigenous people when the explorers began claiming land. Ask them guided questions like, "Indigenous tribes often traveled during different seasons because of the available resources. If they lost access to somewhere with resources they needed, how would that change things?"

Read *(Changes for Indigenous People)*

If your student struggles with understanding diseases, they may benefit from discussing a time when they were sick. Discuss how we have medicines that help us feel better but a long time ago they did not have medicines that would make them feel better or heal them. You can share that smallpox has been eradicated completely, and that influenza and chickenpox are very treatable today.

Read *(Enslavement)*

Help your student understand that enslavement meant the enslaved people were not able to quit working for free for any reason. They belonged to the person who traded for them, like a thing instead of a person. As they consider what this would be like, ask them guiding questions like, "Have you ever felt like you didn't have any control over your life or any choice about something? What did that feel like? What would it be like if life was always like that?"

Learning Styles

Auditory learners may enjoy writing a poem about how Indigenous people interacted with explorers and then reciting the poem to a family member.

Visual learners may enjoy looking at images of the types of shelter European settlers and various Indigenous tribes typically built.

Kinesthetic learners may enjoy visiting an exhibit about European settlement in North America and the lives of Indigenous people during that time.

Extension Activities

Art Exploration

Help your student look up examples of Indigenous people's artwork from 1600–1800. After they have looked at several examples and learned about the materials and designs, allow your student to create their own work of art inspired by what they've seen.

Make Your Own Test

Have students create their own quiz questions about what they have learned from the lesson. This creates a deeper connection to the material and increases retention of the information.

LESSON 74
Explorers and Indigenous People

Answer Key

Write *(How do you think the Indigenous people's lives changed once the early explorers took over their land?)*
Answers will vary. Possible answers: They wouldn't be able to travel to access resources the same way; they might have to change how they eat or what they eat; instead of hunting or planting for just what they need; they needed to grow and hunt extra food to trade, etc.

Write *(Think about the European goods Indigenous people traded for. Why would these items be helpful or useful?)*
Answers will vary. Possible answers: Guns would be useful because it would make work like hunting and getting furs easier; metal cooking utensils could last longer than clay pots, tools like axes would make it much easier to chop and gather firewood, etc.

Show What You Know
1. A
2. True
3. Answers will vary. Possible answers: smallpox, influenza, measles, chickenpox
4. Answers will vary. Possible answers: metal tools, axes, knives, guns, glass, etc.

LESSON 75
Arrival of Explorers

Lesson Objectives

By the end of this lesson, your student will be able to:

- explain ways that the arrival of explorers changed the environment in different areas

Supporting Your Student

Read *(The Age of Exploration)*
Have your student read this section with you and discuss why they think the Age of Exploration is important. If they have any questions about what they are reading, you can read articles online or find books at the library to further their learning about the Age of Exploration.

Online Connection *(European Exploration)*
When watching the European exploration videos with your student, stop often to discuss the roles of the different explorers mentioned and their contributions to the new society. Some questions you could ask are, "What changes did that exploration bring about?" and "Were these positive or negative changes?"

Practice
Help your student research diseases online and discuss whether or not there are vaccines for them and if they are still around. Help your student fill in the chart with three diseases that were cured or that we now have vaccines for.

Learning Styles

Auditory learners may enjoy listening to stories online about explorers in the New World.

Visual learners may enjoy finding pictures of maps and explorers and putting them together on a chart.

Kinesthetic learners may enjoy pretending to be an explorer having a conversation with an Indigenous person about a plant or a new item that they have never seen before.

Extension Activities

Create
Read *The World Made New* by Marc Aronson and help your student create a diorama depicting a village as it was when explorers came. They can use cardboard, molding clay, beads, and any other materials. They can even include toy figures as the people in the villages.

Visit a Virtual Museum
Find a museum that has displays on the Age of Exploration and take a tour with your student. Ask your student what they learned by seeing these villages.

Explore Private and Shared Land
Go online and research the differences between private property and shared land. Ask your student what life would be like today if we shared land instead of owning or renting our own property.

Answer Key

LESSON 75
Arrival of Explorers

Explore
Answers will vary based on your student's interests.

Write *(Explain what happened in colonial America after the overhunting of beavers.)*
Answers will vary. Possible answer: The popularity of beaver-trimmed hats in Europe coupled with Native Americans' desire for European weapons led to the overhunting of beavers in the northeast, and beavers were hunted to extinction. With their loss came the loss of beaver ponds, which had served as habitats for fish as well as water sources for deer, moose, and other animals.

Write *(How did the environment of the Americas suffer from European contact? How did it benefit?)*
Answers will vary. Possible answer: The environment suffered with the introduction of diseases and benefited from plants that could make new medicines.

Practice
Answers will vary based on the chosen diseases.

Show What You Know
1. B
2. C
3. True
4. True
5. Answers will vary. Possible answer: Some changes brought to the New World during the Age of Exploration can include disease, learning about plants, and other changes in the environment brought about by exploration.

LESSON 76
Remembering Explorers

Lesson Objectives

By the end of this lesson, your student will be able to:

- describe ways people remember explorers today, such as memorials, monuments, and holidays

Supporting Your Student

Explore
Take a virtual tour of Mount Rushmore so that your student can experience the vast size and depth of this historical monument.

Read *(Historical Monuments Around the World)*
It would be helpful to go to the public library with your student and find books on memorials and monuments from around the world.

Online Connection
Help your student find monuments of interest online and print photos and articles to refer to when working on the projects in this lesson.

Read *(How Do We Remember Explorers?)*
Read paragraphs with your student and stop for any questions they may have. It may be helpful to have them rephrase key points in their own words. Ask them, "Do you remember learning about some explorers who are remembered today?"

Learning Styles

Auditory learners may enjoy listening to one of the monument tours given by a docent.

Visual learners may enjoy sorting pictures printed from the internet of monuments and memorials from around the world.

Kinesthetic learners may enjoy constructing their favorite monument using blocks, clay, or cardboard.

Extension Activities

Take a Virtual Tour
Go online with your student and search for international tours of monuments and memorials from around the world. Look for tours that include photos and descriptions of each monument or memorial and follow any relevant links to find out more about each.

Create a Poster
After completing a virtual tour of international monuments, have your student pick their favorite monument or memorial. Then have them print photos of the monument or memorial and glue them onto a poster board. They should add the title of their monument or memorial and a sentence description underneath. If possible, your student should also add the location (i.e., city, country, continent).

LESSON 76
Remembering Explorers

Answer Key

Write *(What is a memorial?)*
Answers will vary. Possible answers: A monument is a building or statue that honors something or someone from the past.

Write *(What is a monument?)*
Answers will vary. Possible answers: A way to honor a person, group, or important event from the past. It could be a statue, building, ceremony, or area.

Write *(Why do we celebrate holidays created for people from the past?)*
Answers will vary. Possible answers: Holidays celebrate important events in a country's history.

Write *(How do people celebrate holidays for people they want to remember?)*
Answers will vary. Possible answers: People celebrate holidays for people they remember with days off, parades, and eating specific foods.

Write *(Think about a holiday celebration you went to. Who was it for and how did you celebrate?)*
Answers will vary. Possible answers: going to a party or parade, eating a certain food, listening to music

Write *(What is the location of each of these memorials and celebrations?)*
  1. New York Harbor, United States
  2. Japan
  3. South Dakota, United States
  4. Russia

Practice
Día de Los Muertos: represents a celebration of loved ones who have died

Statue of Liberty: represents freedom and a gift of friendship from the people of France

Columbus Day: represents Christopher Columbus's arrival to the Americas

Mount Rushmore: represents George Washington, Thomas Jefferson, Theodore Roosevelt, and Abraham Lincoln and their invaluable contributions to the United States

Victory Day: represents the surrender of Nazi Germany to the Allies in World War II

Show What You Know
  5. memorial
  6. Holidays
  7. monument
  8. past
  9. stone
  10. Answers will vary based on the monuments your student chose.

LESSON 77
Chapter 8 Review

Lesson Objectives

By the end of this lesson, your student will review the following big ideas from Chapter 8.

- Explorers traveled many places by using tools like a map. (Lessons 70 and 71)
- Explorers faced many challenges while looking for goods to return to their country. (Lessons 71 and 72)
- Explorers and Indigenous people viewed and interacted with land differently. (Lessons 73 and 74)
- Explorers changed the environment in different areas. (Lesson 75)
- People remember explorers with monuments, memorials, and holidays. (Lesson 76)

Supporting Your Student

Review *(Why and How Did Explorers Explore?)*
When reading this section, review with your student the obstacles that explorers faced, the navigation tools they used, and the conditions that were present on the boats they traveled on.

Review *(Explorers Discover Places Around the World)*
Before reading this section, it may help to review some of the explorers who were highlighted throughout this chapter. Ask your student what each explorer did that was important. If your student struggles to remember explorers and what they accomplished, help them review that explorer by referencing earlier lessons in this chapter for review.

Create *(Create a Timeline)*
Help your student organize index cards with at least six explorers. Be sure to write a date on top of each card to make it easier to put in order. Also, be sure that they have explorers from the past and present. If they find more than six explorers, they can draw their timeline on a separate sheet or glue down their index cards in order on a large piece of paper.

Practice *(Venn Diagram)*
Help your student fill in the Venn diagram by first suggesting that one thing both explorers past and present had in common was they were both searching for something. Refer to some past explorers to help them fill out "Explorers Past." Refer to some recent explorers to help them fill out "Explorers Present." Help your student fill in the blanks of the summary.

Learning Styles

Auditory learners may enjoy listening to songs that explorers sang on their journeys or audiobooks on exploration from the past and present.

Visual learners may enjoy finding and printing pictures of explorers from the past and present.

Kinesthetic learners may enjoy creating a ship (for past explorers) or a rocket ship (for present-day explorers) and make a speech as if they were that explorer detailing their journey.

Extension Activities

Create a Timeline
Have your student gather photos of different monuments and memorials around the world and put them in order to create a timeline of historical monuments developed over time.

Visit a Local Museum
Visit a museum (in person or online) that has a display of explorers, memorials, and monuments that represent their discoveries and the changes they brought about in history. If possible, find museums that display discoveries of the explorers that your student chose to include in their timeline.

LESSON 77
Chapter 8 Review

Answer Key

Create *(Create a Timeline)*
Answers will vary but should include some explorers from the past and present in chronological order based on the dates written on the index cards.

Practice *(Vocabulary)*
Drawings will vary. Check your student's drawings to ensure they have a firm understanding of each word.

Practice *(Venn Diagram)*
Answers will vary. Possible answers:

Explorers Past: were looking to discover new lands, wanted to create new societies, brought back resources to their own country

Explorers Present: are looking to expand current societies that are underdeveloped, are looking to discover places away from Earth

Both: were looking to discover new things

Write
1. John Cabot
2. Bartolomeu Dias
3. Francisco Coronado
4. explorers
5. wealthy
6. Indigenous

Write *(What were some difficulties explorers faced?)*
Answers will vary. Possible answer: Explorers faced difficulties with longer boat rides, diseases from pests, waves, and food spoilage.

CHAPTER 8
Assessment

Quick Review

Refer to the statement your student circled in the Show What You Know section to self-assess their knowledge of the chapter concepts. Then to assist in determining if your student is ready to take the assessment, consider:

- Having your student ask questions they have about explorers.
- Having your student write a summary comparing and contrasting two explorers from the past and present.
- Having your student prepare a timeline that shows the events and accomplishments of different explorers.

CHAPTER 8
Assessment

Chapter Assessment

Project: An Explorer's Speech

Choose one explorer from the chapter.

Project Requirements:

As you research, be sure to answer the following:

- Where is the explorer from, and where did they go?
- What was the explorer's motivation for exploration?
- What did they hope to gain from their expedition?
- What did they learn there about society?
- What did they bring back to their own land?

Write a speech from the explorer's perspective, explaining their journey and findings to their home country. Include answers to questions in your speech.

Present your speech to your instructor.

CHAPTER 8
Assessment

Chapter Assessment Rubric

Use the following rubric to grade your student's assessment.

	4	3	2	1	Points
Connection to the Chapter	The speech includes all components and is connected to the chapter.	The speech includes most components and is somewhat connected to the chapter.	The speech includes some components and is somewhat connected to the chapter.	The speech does not include any components and is not connected to the chapter.	
Presentation	The presenter speaks loudly and clearly and maintains eye contact throughout the presentation.	The presenter speaks loudly and clearly but does not make consistent eye contact with the audience.	The presenter uses frequent filler words and is somewhat unclear. The presenter does not make consistent eye contact.	The presenter's speech is difficult to comprehend and unclear.	
Grammar and Mechanics	The speech is clear and grammatically correct.	The speech is mostly clear with one or two grammar errors.	The speech is somewhat clear with several grammar errors.	The speech has a distracting number of grammar errors.	

Total Points _____/12

Average _____

Discover! SOCIAL STUDIES • GRADE 2 • CHAPTER 8 ASSESSMENT

CHAPTER 8
Assessment

Alternative Assessment

It is recommended that the instructor provides the student with support during the assessment to include reading and explaining directions, reading any unknown words or phrases, allowing the student to provide verbal responses that are then recorded, and allowing the student to complete sections of the assessment over the course of the day(s).

Match each word with its definition.

1. _____ disease
2. _____ journey
3. _____ own
4. _____ challenge
5. _____ discover
6. _____ steward
7. _____ explorer
8. _____ claim
9. _____ expedition
10. _____ enslaved person

A. a difficult task or problem
B. a sickness that keeps the body from working
C. to manage or look after
D. an act of traveling from one place to another
E. someone who travels to places
F. someone who is owned by another person
G. to have something as property
H. to be the first to find out or see something
I. a journey or voyage taken by a group of people
J. to say that something belongs to you

CHAPTER 8
Assessment

Alternative Assessment Answer Key

1. B
2. D
3. G
4. A
5. H
6. C
7. E
8. J
9. I
10. F